150 Home Plans

Ranch
Expansion Ranch
Vacation and Leisure Homes
Dome Homes

Designs by William G. Chirgotis, Architect

Library of Congress Catalogue Card Number 81-67298

ISBN 0-932944-48-5 Paperback

Printed in the United States of America

CONTENTS

WHY AN ARCHITECT DESIGNED HOME?

Because an architect is seldom consulted by the average family, his is a little-understood profession. Most people only think of an architect as man who designs skyscrapers, factories, churches, schools, and other massive structures. Few realize that the majority of architects use their talent to solve rural and suburban residential problems. These are the problems the average family faces when the members plan to build a new home. So few families realize this fact that less than 5% of them start their planning by visiting an architect. The other 95% visit a model home built in a development or perhaps buy blueprints from a stock plan service. Either way, they may still be receiving, indirectly, the benefit of architectural talent, if the model or the stock plan represents the work of an architect. A house designed by an architect will certainly give the potential homeowner a better layout, superior design, and best dollar value.

If you intend to use stock, or predesigned plans to construct your home, be sure that they are the work of a reputable architect. Because the blueprints of the homes in this book are available at a small fraction of their original cost, thousands of families who build from our plans enjoy a better standard of living. Avoid plans that bear the name of a designer but not an architect. The largest investment of your lifetime deserves the insurance of an architect's name.

In many sections of the country, there are no architects available within reach. Even in outlying sections of major cities, architects are often too busy to be available for small home work. If this is the case, you will undoubtedly consider purchasing a stock plan. A stock plan is a home design that is already in the form of working drawings. By permitting a home design to be published, the architect makes the plan available to many families. The plans cost them only a fraction of the original cost. They receive copies of substantially the identical blueprints from which the original house was constructed. There may even be some improvements and refinements that resulted from the experience gained in building the original home. If you do employ an architect, one or more stock plans can serve as a starting point for your discussions, helping to crystallize your ideas and accelerate the planning. If the plan you buy is architect-designed, you can be certain that when it is properly executed by a competent builder, you are going to be the proud owner of a home which is solidly built, space-engineered, comfort-endowed, and esthetically appealing. In short, you insure your investment by getting the maximum house per dollar spent. The homes illustrated in this book have layouts suited to a great variety of families all over the country and in most income brackets. As you leaf through the portfolios which follow, you will see many homes that you feel you have seen and admired before. It is quite likely that you have driven past them and envied their lucky owners. They all exist. They are now available to you.

It is the aim of this book to display the home designs of one of this country's leading architects, William G. Chirgotis, to make these homes available to the home-building public, and to point out how architectural services can help any family to attain a home which meets their aspirations.

A GUIDE TO ASSIST YOU IN SELECTING A HOME DESIGN TO FIT YOUR NEEDS

Of the many homes illustrated in this plan book, one is certain to be your "Dream Home" meeting your budget and family requirements. The question is: which one?

The answer, of course, depends on a number of factors. Some are personal considerations; others are basic needs. Still others are financial. You must analyze each design on all points.

Number of Rooms:

If financially feasible, it is a good idea to provide separate bedrooms for each child and at least two bathrooms if there is more than one child. If a grandparent lives with you, another separate bedroom with private bath is essential.

Style:

The matter of style depends on personal preference or taste. However, it is unwise to build a home radically "different" from the other homes in a neighborhood.

Type:

Each house type has its own advantages. The one-story ranch allows for easy living and maintenance. The two-story and 1½ story Cape Cod cost less per square foot and have complete separation of entertainment and sleeping areas. The split-level and multi-level combine features of both.

Multi-Level

Sometimes called Hi-ranch or Bi-level, this type of house has a front foyer at ground level and a stairway up to the main living area and another down to what would ordinarily be the basement. The basement is raised enough to permit windows above ground, and the area usually contains a recreation or informal room.

Split-Level

This type features three or four levels. The living and bedroom areas are separated, but the flights of stairs are shorter than in a two-story. Split-levels are suitable for rolling terrain. They require more land than a two-story, but have more livable space on the same land than a ranch.

Two-Story

On the basis of cost per square foot, a two-story is usually lower than other houses. The upstairs bedrooms have more privacy. More rooms can be built on less land than with any other type.

Ranches

Possibly the most popular type home today, the ranch home offers the advantage of ease of living and maintenance, all on one floor. With proper planning and design, specialized living areas can be created easily by utilizing one wing of the home for sleeping and the other portion for daytime and living activities.

Expansion Ranches

The expansion ranch is often called a 1½-story house. This team means the attic can be finished at the time of construction or later on. This plan often features a master bedroom on the first floor and children's bedrooms upstairs. Most 1½-story houses have traditional details in the Cape Cod style.

Vacation and Leisure-Time Homes

Whatever your taste or budget, the included designs for vacation or leisure-time living offer a change from everyday living. Today many Americans are investing in a "second" home; it pays dividends in pleasure and relaxation and increase in value over the years.

Dome Homes

This unique concept of living introduced about twenty years ago, is enjoying phenomenal popularity today.

Technically, the dome home originated from the sphere, nature's most efficient means of enclosing space economically. The dome is more popular in times of inflation and ever-increasing construction costs because the factory-assembled, triangular frames are simply bolted together on the site to form the finished building. Drastic reductions are possible on quantities of building materials and on-site labor costs. A dome home can cost as much as 20 percent less than conventional housing, and it has been established that heating, cooling, and insurance costs can be reduced by at least 30%.

The dome provides a living area which also answers the need for efficient energy consumption, and is particularly adaptable to solar heating. Today's dome homes are attractive and offer an exciting new way of living.

HOW TO READ A FLOOR PLAN

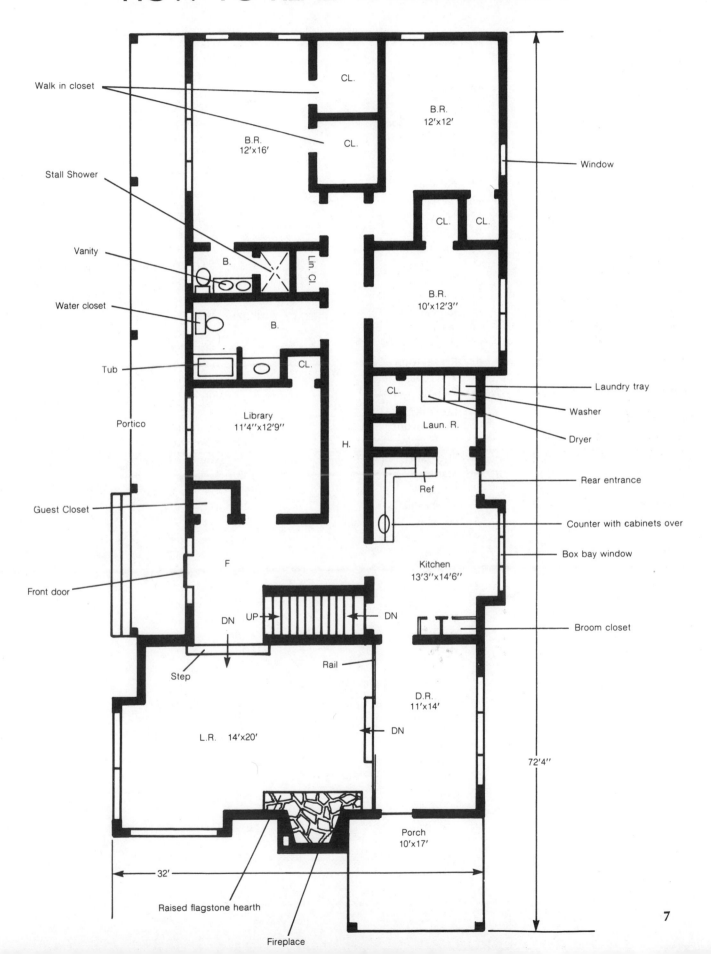

Walk in closet

Stall Shower

Vanity

Water closet

Tub

Portico

Guest Closet

Front door

Step

CL.

B.R.
12'x16'

CL.

B.

Lin. Cl.

B.

CL.

Library
11'4''x12'9''

H.

F

DN   UP

Rail

L.R.   14'x20'

Raised flagstone hearth

Fireplace

B.R.
12'x12'

CL.   CL.

B.R.
10'x12'3''

CL.

Laun. R.

Ref

Kitchen
13'3''x14'6''

DN

D.R.
11'x14'

DN

Porch
10'x17'

Window

Laundry tray

Washer

Dryer

Rear entrance

Counter with cabinets over

Box bay window

Broom closet

72'4''

32'

INDEX

RANCHES

RANCH

An all-inclusive word that covers virtually any house in which all the rooms are on one floor at ground level. Because of the general truth that it costs more to build horizontally than vertically, the cost of a ranch, on the basis of the amount per square foot, is usually higher. The maintenance of a ranch is easier. Stair climbing is non-existent or minimal.

The Middleton

The front entrance of this graceful ranch home opens into a vestibule with a guest closet. The living room, immediately to one side of the entrance, has a large picture window. The kitchen is located at the rear of the home. It has access both to a porch designed for leisure activities and to the formal dining room. The dining room location allows conversion to a third bedroom or a den with no trouble or inconvenience to the family.

TOTAL LIVING AREA: 1,066 sq. ft.

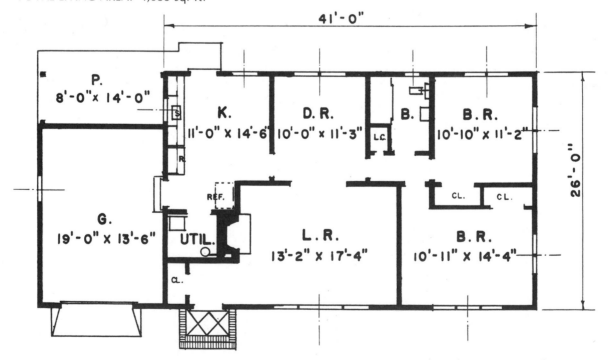

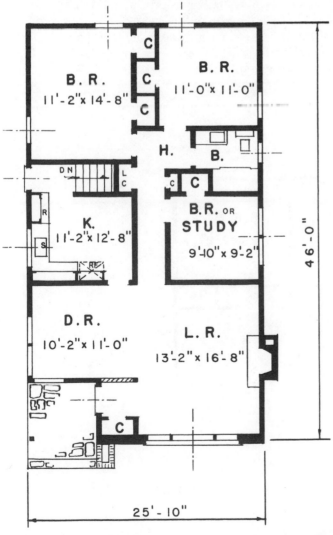

The Newton

It is often difficult to find a home plan for an attractive and fully functional one-story house that is well designed and still scaled to fit on a 50- or even a 40-foot lot, as this home is. If you study the plan carefully, you immediately will discover a home that meets the requirements of a narrow lot, and becomes a very attractive addition to any neighborhood.

The interior of this home contains a large living room with a dining L, a full-sized kitchen, and three bedrooms. The sheltered entryway welcomes visitors to this appealing home.

TOTAL LIVING AREA: 1,140 sq. ft.

The Califon

This economical and compact two-bedroom ranch home has excellent features in its plan. The design is compact in appearance and belies the size of the rooms. A glance at the plan reveals the dimensions of the large living room and the size of the spacious kitchen. The service entrance is well located, provides direct access to the basement, and includes a door for convenient serving and entertaining on the porch. Any family will find living and working in this wonderful ranch home to be a constant pleasure.

TOTAL LIVING AREA: 1,180 sq. ft. excluding the porch

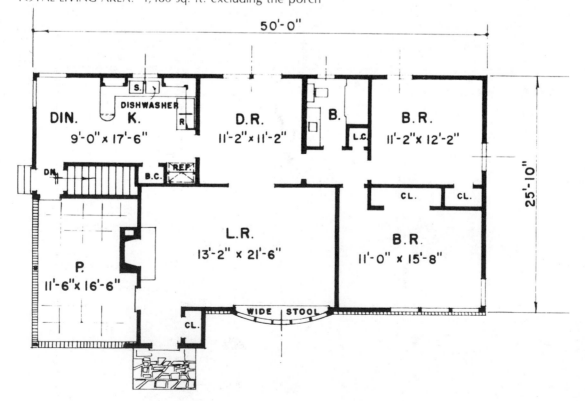

FIRST FLOOR PLAN

The Maywood

To many, the ranch home has become the ideal design for comfortable and gracious living. Originally, the ranch style was exclusively a large sprawling house; however, in city and suburban areas with serious lot size limitations, such a layout usually is not practical.

The ranch style, for this purpose, has been condensed. This house in particular has been planned so that by eliminating or detaching the garage and moving the porch to the rear, it can be built on a lot as small as 50 feet wide.

Look at all the features this home contains: (1) interior entry hall; (2) through passage to the kitchen; (3) separated sleeping and living areas; (4) large closet areas; (5) large living room with a real fireplace; (6) a spacious kitchen and dining area with snack bar; (7) protected passage across the porch to the attached garage.

Unquestionably, with minimum expense, this plan affords the maximum in efficiency and comfort of living for the whole family.

TOTAL LIVING AREA: 1,185 sq. ft. excluding the porch and garage

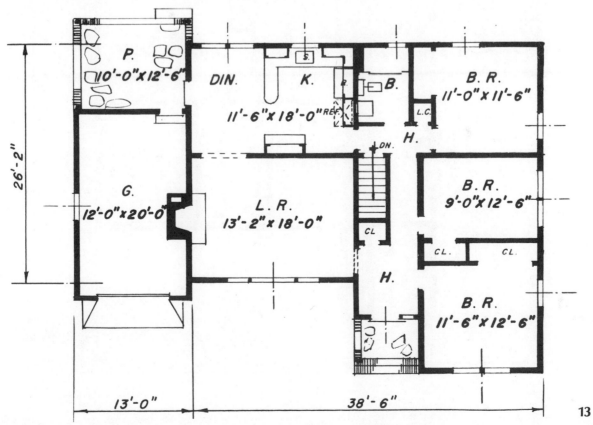

The Willow

The brick and wood shingle exterior on this home combines with the interior layout to create a cozy and comfortable ranch house. This home has all the privacy of second floor bedrooms without any stair climbing.

The large "L" shape living and dining room provides a spacious area usually found only in larger and more expensive houses. You also will appreciate the covered entrance platform, especially when fumbling for your key on any rainy evening.

There is extensive sink and work area in the kitchen, 22 square feet of it, plus cabinet space. An alcove corner may become a built-in breakfast nook or a lunch bar.

A separate entrance vestibule means that the living room will always be free of cold drafts. The vestibule also provides a convenient guest closet. Fill the entrance planting box with your favorite flowers and this house will become the house of your very own dreams.

TOTAL LIVING AREA: 1,196 sq. ft.

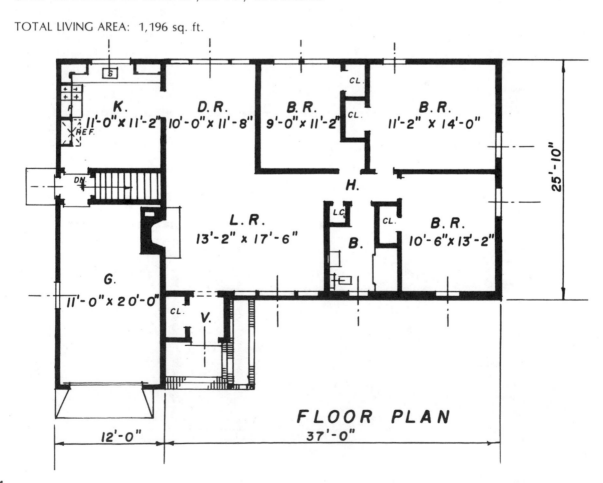

FLOOR PLAN

The Oakhurst

Here is a two-bedroom ranch with straight, clean lines. Although it seems to have a tremendous amount of living area, this home contains only 1,200 square feet of habitable space, including the greenhouse. However, good traffic flow and planning provide for all the needs of a family that wants all the rooms on one floor.

The entry gives the visitor a view of both the living room and the dining room, extending the illusion of spaciousness. To the left is the living room, 22 feet 9 inches in length, with a full picture window that can be the center of decorating interest.

Simple to construct and economical to build, this plan provides the design for a house that will be pleasant and comfortable for the small family with a limited budget.

TOTAL LIVING AREA: First floor   1,114 sq. ft.
                                Garage   280 sq. ft.
                                Greenhouse   86 sq. ft.

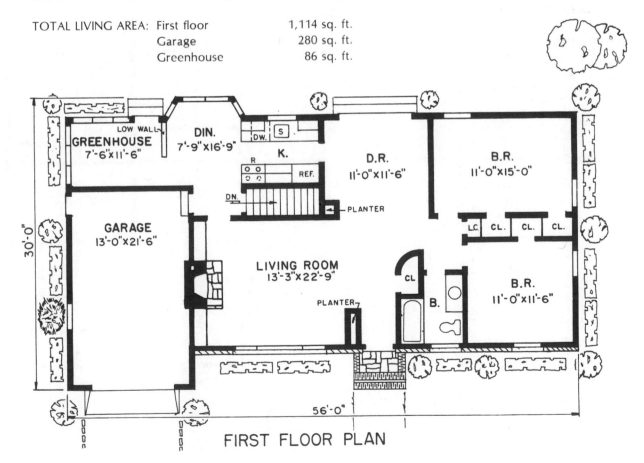

FIRST FLOOR PLAN

The Fielding

This beautiful home that makes the maximum use of every single inch of floor space is designed for those of you with a relatively narrow lot.

The entrance hall includes a handy closet. From the entrance, the passage allows people who enter the front door to go directly to the kitchen without having to pass through either the large living room or the dining room. This is only one of the many positive features of this cozy home; others will be revealed by giving a rapid survey to the floor plan.

From the step-saving kitchen to the many closets, this home plan meets standards and brings you conveniences that are usually associated with much larger homes.

TOTAL LIVING AREA: 1,204 sq. ft.

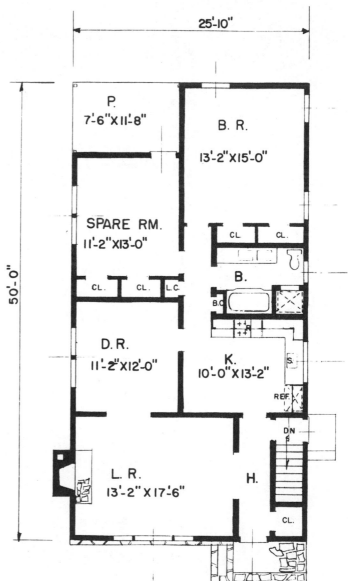

The Douglas

A scanning of the layout of this unusual, L-shaped ranch home plan will reveal something a little different. There is a one car garage and a breezeway that combine to provide a convenient circulation pattern. This plan also features an attractive, informal kitchen-family room.

TOTAL LIVING AREA: 1,220 sq. ft. excluding porch and garage

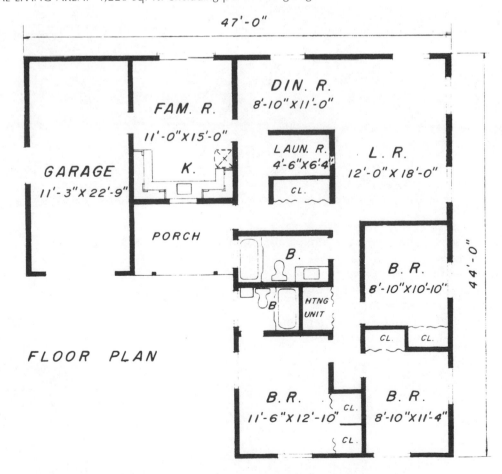

FLOOR PLAN

The Tilford

Long and low, this economical ranch home is stretched across the front for that "large-house" look. In spite of its length this is not an expensive house, yet contains all of the features found in many homes of much greater size and cost. A flagstone fireplace hearth extends to the front entrance to form a small entry area which includes a large guest closet. The living-dining ell is extra large and provides large wall areas for decoration and furniture arrangement. An ample kitchen provides dining space at the windows and has a separate small foyer at the service entrance which also leads down to the basement.

The three bedrooms are well separated from the living area and in addition to being served by one full sized bath, there is also a small private lavatory off the Master bedroom.

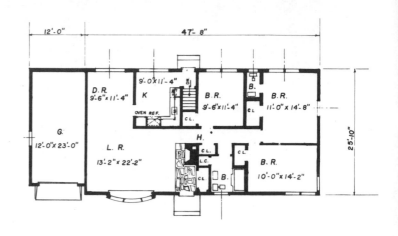

TOTAL LIVING AREA: 1,230 sq. ft. (excluding garage)

The Sutton

This three-bedroom ranch design derives its eye-catching character through its centrally located landscaped atrium, the three walls of which are almost completely glass and help bring an outdoor atmosphere into the house.

Inside, — a flagstone paved foyer effectively zones the activity areas; — the kitchen to the right, the dining-living area straight ahead and the small hallway around the perimeter of the atrium facilitates the flow of traffic to the other rooms.

If convenient and comfortable living is of primary importance in your search for a new contemporary ranch design with an outdoor atmosphere — this could be just the thing.

TOTAL LIVING AREA: 1,250 sq. ft.
    Atrium   255 sq. ft.
    Garage   529 sq. ft.

The Homewood

Prospective home builders have made this one of the most popular ranch home designs available today.

This house has two cozy bedrooms convenient to the full bath. The step-saving kitchen has been well designed to give easy access to the dining area and, for those more formal occasions, to the adjoining dining room. As an added bonus, there is a homey den that may also serve as a TV room.

TOTAL LIVING AREA. 1,314 sq. ft.

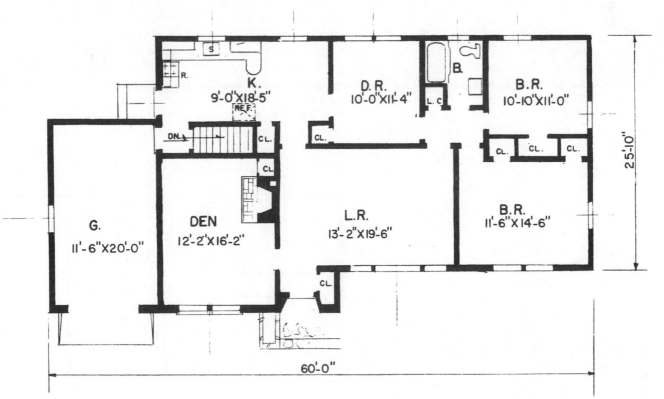

The Neptune

If you're just starting out in life, and can't afford a big new home—but still want to enjoy the very real benefits of home ownership and want to build a basic, comfortable house with the proper blend of economy and style—you would do well to consider this three bedroom design.

Inside, the architect has utilized every inch of the 1,275 square feet of living space; there seems to be a tremendous amount of habitable area in a house of this size, with everything needed by a family of two, three or four that wants all the rooms on one floor.

There is no doubt that the "all-on-one-floor" living of this clean and simple design is also especially appealing to retired couples or busy mothers of small families.

TOTAL LIVING AREA: 1,275 sq. ft.

The Stanford

Families with an "in with the new, out with the old" philosophy of life will be attracted to this clean-lined contemporary three bedroom ranch design with its dramatic use of glass and unique roof lines.

The foyer is separated from the living room by a decorative wrought iron railing. This feature and the beamed cathedral ceiling of the living room visually enlarge this area.

This exquisite contemporary ranch design that is planned to achieve both economy and convenience and has all the ingredients of a larger home; it is ideal for a first home for young families or as a retirement home for mature couples.

TOTAL LIVING AREA: 1,306 sq. ft.
Garage   254 sq. ft.

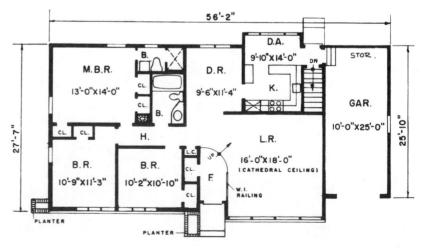

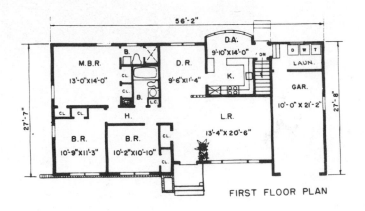

FIRST FLOOR PLAN

The Thayer

This rather unusual ranch style plan offers many special features in a home designed for a relatively narrow lot. In some areas, this home could be built on a lot as narrow as 45 feet if the breezeway and garage were omitted. A long sheltered patio, complete with a barbecue, is located on the side of the house. This area is screened for privacy by a front wall.

The interior has plenty of closet space for the three bedrooms and for extras. The bright kitchen offers ample work and storage space and includes a large corner area suitable for breakfast and lunch dining. Entrance to the full basement is directly adjacent to the outside kitchen door.

A vestibule separates the well protected main entrance from the large L-shaped living-dining areas and the attached breezeway provides protected access to the garage in all weather.

Another fine feature of this home is the living room fireplace, which serves as a decorating focus.

TOTAL LIVING AREA: 1,352 sq. ft. excluding porch and garage

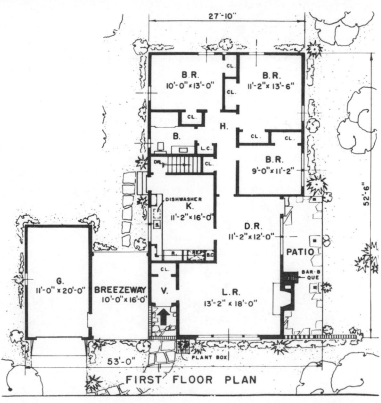

FIRST FLOOR PLAN

The Granada

The Spanish flavor of the old Southwest is delightfully captured and comes to life in the form of this enchanting ranch.

An interesting treatment of mixing rough stucco finish, projecting stained wood beams, arched picture window, low pitched roofs and stone-veneer, lends an exotic air of a Spanish villa to this latest design.

Inside,—the areas are planned for easy living, from the central entrance, you can reach any room with a minimum of steps from the small but adequate foyer which serves as an efficient traffic control center. A decorative wrought iron railing separates the foyer from the living room to the right. This feature and the beamed cathedral ceiling of the living room enlarge the entire area.

The bedroom area has three bedrooms clustered around a minumum hallway and is clearly delineated to maximum privacy and good sound conditioning with a buffer zone of closets and bathrooms.

This design modeled after the one-floor rambling structures built in the open spaces of the west can be a source of pride in any neighborhood.

TOTAL LIVING AREA: 1320 sq. ft.
    Basement   1320 sq. ft.
    Garage   550 sq. ft.

The Richmond

The ideal ranch plan for many is one which is planned around a center hall, with rooms easily accessible. With this plan you have the privacy and comfort of a 2 story house combined with the gracious ease of ranch house living. To the right of the entrance hall is a 20' living room opening freely in the popular "L" shape to a full-size dining room. Large window areas front and rear in these rooms add both light and through ventilation to this spacious entertaining area.

There's a large kitchen with ample work counter, and space enough for a table for breakfast and the children's lunch too. The bedroom wing is separated enough to lend privacy and quiet for the children's rooms, and each bedroom has large sliding-door closet space.

The open porch in back of the garage is a wonderful asset for summer evenings, and the over-size garage provides space for the car and plenty of storage for all garden tools and children's outdoor toys.

TOTAL LIVING AREA: 1,336 sq. ft. (excl. porch
   & garage)

The Kilmer

A refreshing exterior is boasted by this popular ranch design which will make it a hit in any neighborhood.

Including three airy bedrooms, a modern kitchen and the combination living-dining room, the interior comes to a graceful conclusion at a friendly terrace which is found at the rear of this breath taking home.

TOTAL LIVING AREA: 1,320 sq. ft.

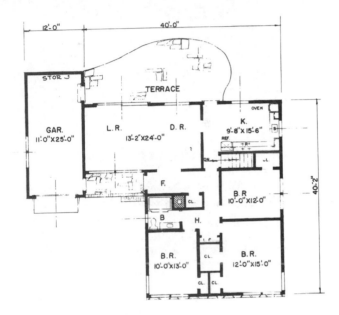

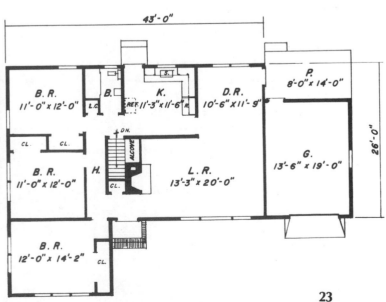

The Oaklynn

An eyecatching brick planter draws the attention as a visitor moves from the driveway across to the entrance of this charming and functional ranch home.

The ample foyer contains an immense sliding door closet for the convenience of the family and guests and is directly adjacent to the guest lavatory and the den to the right. Just a few steps toward the rear of the house is a door leading to a kitchen that would be any housewife's dream. The efficient U-shape of the work space provides extensive counter and cabinets. The spacious bay window at the end of the kitchen becomes a cheery space for a dinette.

The L-shape arrangement of the living and dining areas gives an open feeling appropriate to modern living. There are large glassed areas in the rear wall that open onto a terrace to combine indoor and outdoor dining in the contemporary style.

The two bedrooms are provided with ample closet space and flank the main bath for convenience.

TOTAL LIVING AREA: 1,400 sq. ft. excluding garage and terrace

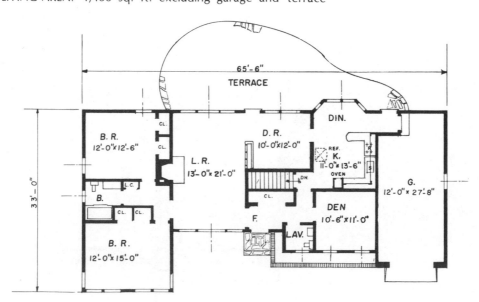

The Huntington

A graceful living room with an unusual fireplace, an inviting dining room, and an efficient kitchen with a large dining space are the highlights of the plan for this friendly looking home. The three bedrooms, which are convenient to the bathroom, each contain plentiful closet space and are designed to provide comfortable living space and a maximum expanse of windows. A covered porch, meant to be floored in flagstone, connects the garage and the living-dining areas.

The exterior is accented by a variety of finish materials and the design is completed by a stone planting box that runs next to the entry and along the living room window wall.

TOTAL LIVING AREA: 1,425 sq. ft.

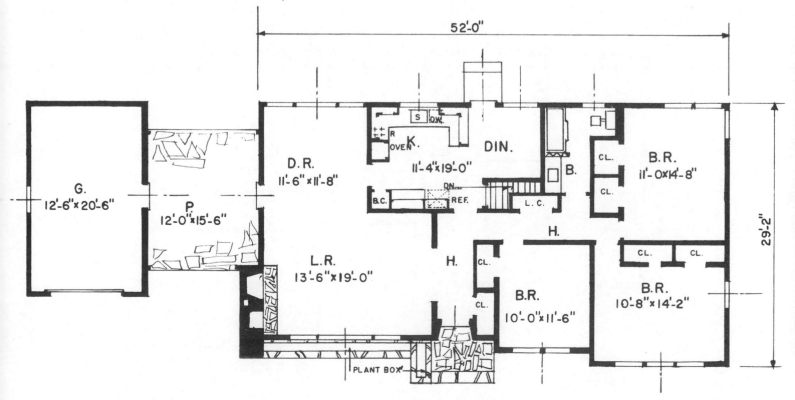

The Barton

Three ample bedrooms, each with roomy closets, and two full baths are the features of the secluded slumber area of this popular ranch design.

The living and dining rooms form an expansive L that is ideal for entertaining and relaxing. The back entry is near the generously sized kitchen. The entry is large enough to provide space for full laundry facilities.

TOTAL LIVING AREA: 1,430 sq. ft.

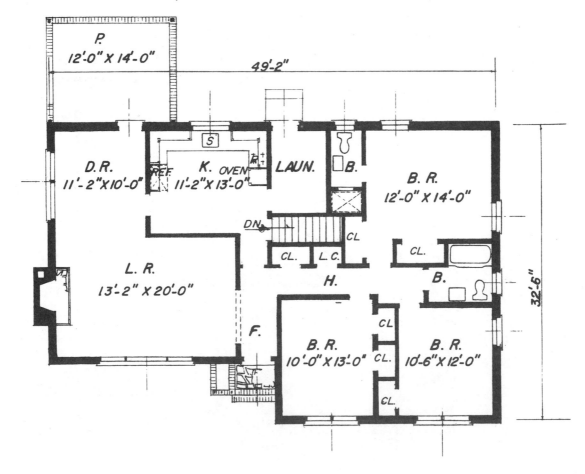

The Anderson

Here is a house planned to be a dream home come true. It is bright, with full view windows in the living and dining areas, as well as in the kitchen and breakfast nook. The smaller bedroom has two exposures, but at the front, the master bedroom has even more windows, with two corners and nearly all the intervening wall opened with glass. These windows are set high to allow for the best ventilation and to retain privacy. All closets in this house are king-size, but the dressing room-closet in the master suite deserves special mention. It is large enough so that part of it could be turned into a lavatory at a future date. The master bedroom also has a built-in vanity to pamper the woman of the house. Kitchen chores will be handled quickly in that efficient room, which is planned to save time and many steps. The laundry room, in the most convenient location, has access to a drying yard and is close to the basement stairs. Built-in bookcases frame the fireplace in the huge living room. A plant shelf at the entry combines beauty and practicality.

TOTAL LIVING AREA: 1,460 sq. ft.

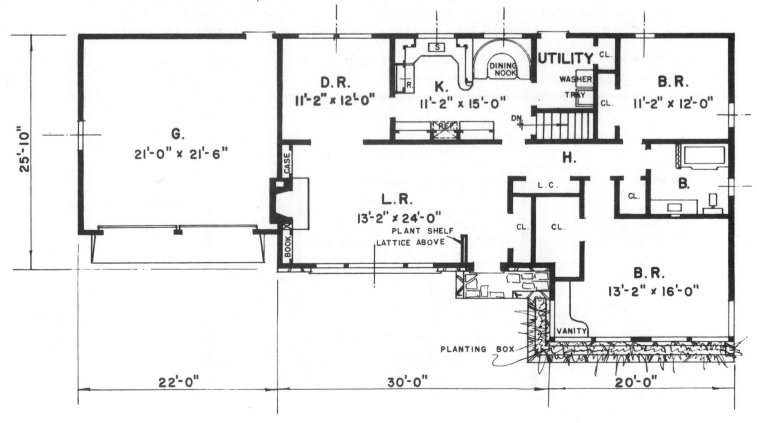

The Sheridan

A home with a view is always appealing. If your property does not have an attractive street-side view, this plan presents a desirable alternative.

This house is designed so that the living room and dining room, both spacious, and the breezeway are all open to the rear. This allows you to landscape and to screen your rear yard to create the view you want. The home is not deep from front to back, so you should be able to enjoy a view of a generously proportioned backyard.

The kitchen is adjacent to the breezeway, which means easy serving of summer snacks or suppers, and to the front entrance for quick response to callers.

TOTAL LIVING AREA: 1,475 sq. ft. excluding porch and garage

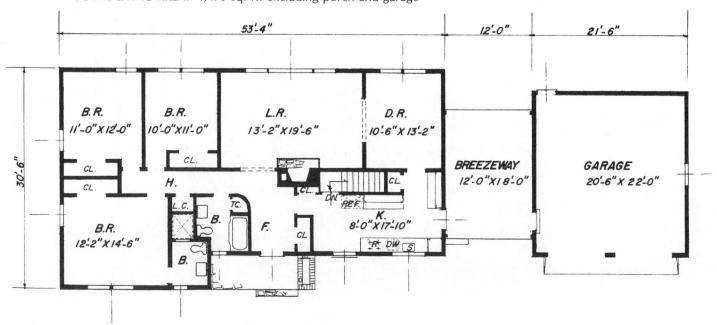

The Edmonton

The entrance to this three-bedroom, contemporary ranch is accented by a large, L-shaped brick planter. When it is planted with flowers and shrubs, it will welcome your visitors. The entrance foyer serves as more than the starting point of good traffic circulation; it creates an excellent first impression of the house. Decorative wrought iron railings separate the foyer from the living room at the left.

Excellent decorating possibilities abound in the sunken living room, which has a log-burning corner brick-faced fireplace, corner windows and extensive wall space.

The spartan simplicity of this contemporary design meets the demands for convenience and ease of maintenance required by many families. This home will be appropriate in any surrounding and in any part of the country.

TOTAL LIVING AREA: First floor   1,490 sq. ft.
                          Basement   1,490 sq. ft.
                          Garage   300 sq. ft.

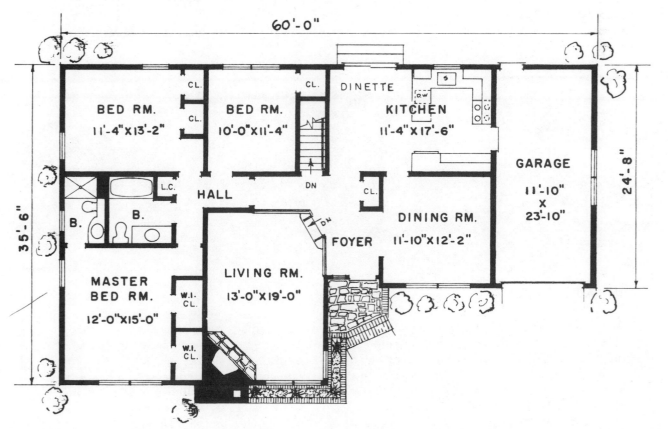

The Leeds

The shape of this modern design three bedroom ranch is in the form of an "L" which enables it to fit on a smaller lot than if all the rooms were placed within a conventional ranch outline.

It is enhanced by the horizontally-paned corner windows, stone veneer and the V-joint boarding in the gable that follows the roof pitch.

TOTAL LIVING AREA: 1,430 sq. ft.

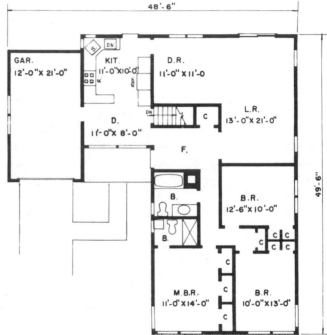

The Marlboro

Here is a modern ranch style home that has made a hit with so many prospective home owners.

There are three cozy, yet spacious bedrooms, each containing more than ample closet space. Convenient to your bedroom there are 1½ well designed baths.

The full size living room directly off the entry hall opens through an archway into a beautiful dining room. There is direct accessibility into the cheery and convenient kitchen from the dining room and from the entry hall.

A relaxing breeze-way and roomy garage round out this design for contented living.

TOTAL LIVING AREA: 1,434 sq. ft.

The Glenview

The "Glenview" is a home for living, for entertaining and for comfort. It will delight in receiving your guests into its cheery spacious atmosphere. The large flagstone floored foyer with generous guest closet, short divider wall and attractive planter will usher you into an enormous area for living and dining. It is open from the front picture window to the rear glass wall and set off by the centrally located fireplace with its interesting free form hearth.

The kitchen will accept with pleasure your praises for its spaciousness; its multitude of cabinets and generous work top areas, plus the separate dinette area.

With cool quiet the three bedrooms will offer solitude and comfort for your sleeping hours; ample and convenient storage space for your wardrobe and modern efficiency, privacy and beauty for your toiletry in either of two full baths.

TOTAL LIVING AREA: 1,470 sq. ft. (excl. garage.)

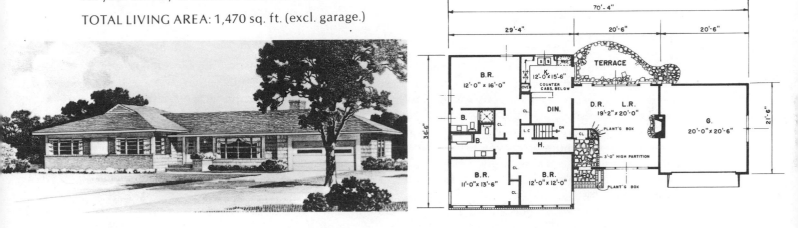

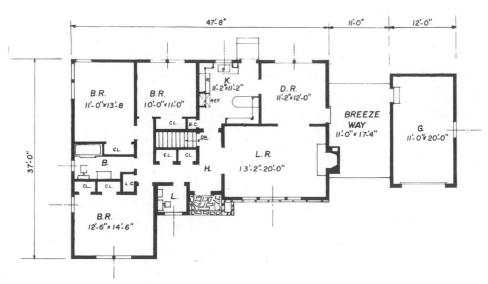

· FIRST FLOOR PLAN ·

The Channing

In today's housing world, more and more families are looking for homes that are economical, yet distinctive and attractive enough to take real pride in ownership. This contemporary three bedroom ranch design, with shadow box windows and natural wood siding applied vertically on the exterior has a floor plan that many young families will find much to their liking.

The bedroom area has three bedrooms clustered around a minumum hallway and is clearly delineated for maximum privacy. A private bath services the master bedroom that has the quiet rear corner of the house. There are two closets, one of which is a walk-in, and a vanity in the dressing area. To the front are the other two bedrooms, for children or guests, with excellent wall space and double closets.

This contemporary ranch planned for both economy and convenience is ideal for a first home for young families or as a retirement home for mature couples.

TOTAL LIVING AREA: 1,483 sq. ft.
Garage: 550 sq. ft.

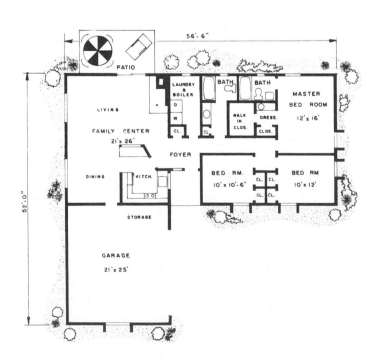

The Larchmont

This spacious six room ranch home has many features expressly designed for your comfort. Note the front entrance protected from the weather on two sides and overhead by the large roof projection. There is a through hall leading directly from the entrance to the kitchen, and the kitchen itself is spacious, with enough room for table and chairs. A large porch off the dining room with access to the garage provides ample sitting area and convenient serving for outdoor dining.

Notice the "L" shaped dining-living room, giving the advantages of the modern open plan, yet providing ample wall space for convenient furniture arrangement.

You will live graciously and well in this home with its private master bedroom, shower bath and enormous double closets. Note that the bedroom lighting is by many high windows, a typical ranch style feature providing ample wall space below for furniture and beds.

TOTAL LIVING AREA: 1,506 sq. ft.

The Oakdale

This unusual three-bedroom two-bath ranch home incorporates the new and increasingly popular arrangement of living and dining rooms in the rear. Combining the best features of the conventional home and the newest in modern living, this plan will prove to you, upon examination, that nothing surpasses our modern day planning for economy and convenience of living.

TOTAL LIVING AREA: 1,515 sq. ft. (excluding porch
& garage)

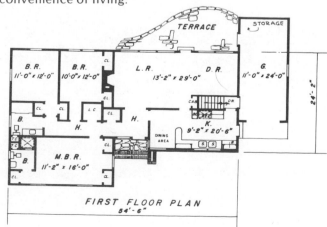

FIRST FLOOR PLAN
54'-6"

The Barrett

Family comfort counts in this spacious ranch house. Large rooms are featured with each of the three bedrooms "master" sized. The closets are tremendous and there are plenty of them. The economy of back-to-back plumbing affords luxury of a full family bathroom including a vanity powder room alcove as well as a private shower bathroom for the parents' bedroom . A skillfully planned kitchen includes a breakfast alcove which could be curtained to make a full room. The entertaining "L" formed by the living and dining rooms and the family room makes indoor-outdoor living a joy and wonderful windows bring summer breezes and winter sunshine in.

TOTAL LIVING AREA: 1,530 sq. ft. excluding garage.

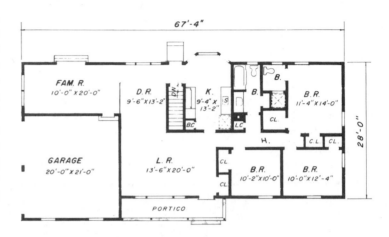

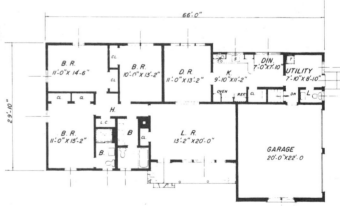

The Lawrence

The warm exterior lines of this ranch plan stand ready to extend a welcome to the family whose home it will become.

All rooms are sized for comfort and arranged for convenience. The utility room at the rear corner serves multi-purpose as laundry room, mud room and foyer area from outside, garage and basement.

There is an abundance of work counter and cabinet space in the kitchen as well as a pantry closet and separate dinette space.

The master bedroom has its private bath and the hall bath is separated into two areas for multi use.

Closet space in all three bedrooms is ample, and in addition, there are a large linen closet in the hall and a guest closet at the entrance.

TOTAL LIVING AREA: 1,540 sq. ft.

The Ridgewood

This compact ranch style home embodies all the features of its larger sprawling prototype, yet is small enough to fit on the average suburban lot. There are three spacious bedrooms and two well-designed baths. Note the tremendous closet space, particularly the large walk-in type in the master bedroom. The entry-hall closet has plenty of room for family wraps and guest's wraps with no crowding. A very desirable feature is the vestibule entry. Recessed for weather protection, it affords a buffer area for cold winds and wet feet. Note that the kitchen is directly accessible from the hall—which means no traffic through living and dining rooms. There are plenty of work counter areas in this kitchen, lots of cabinets above and below and an alcove corner for breakfasts and lunches. The extra wide living room directly off the entry hall opens through an archway into a spacious dining room which in turn connects the kitchen and porch for convenient serving on summer evenings.

TOTAL LIVING AREA: 1,571 sq. ft. (excl. porch & garage)

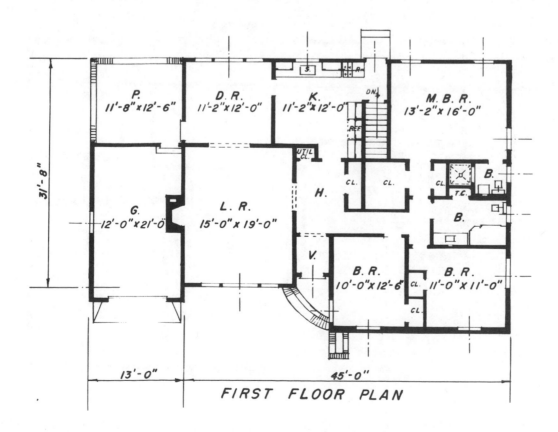

FIRST FLOOR PLAN

The Melrose

Today a ranch home is the dream of many. This plan may be the perfect answer to those dreams for you and your family. The kitchen is located to the left of the foyer. This kitchen has a near-perfect layout that provides family dining space. Behind this room we find a large dining-living room that opens out to the patio beyond. This home features a two-car garage, extra closet space and cross-ventilation in the bedrooms.

TOTAL LIVING AREA: 1,500 sq. ft.

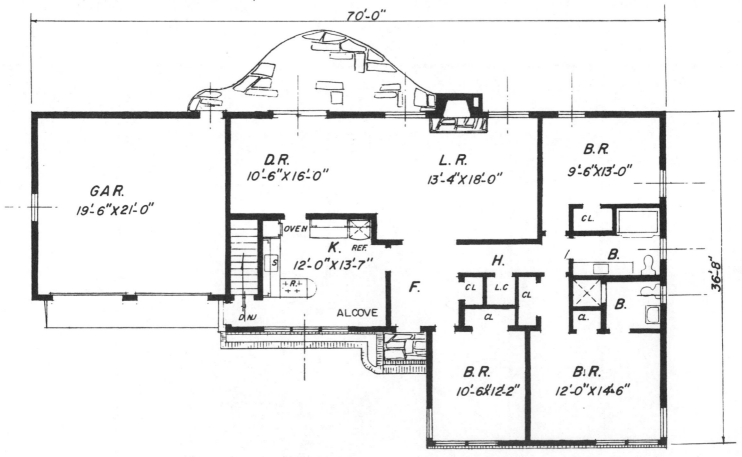

The Montecito

Many architectural details found on the exterior of this design are typically Spanish. The smooth stucco walls, heavy oak paneled door, curved clay top chimneys, arched garage doors and the rugged wood beams emphasize the roof and give it a pleasing sweep.

A wrought iron gate opens on the arcade walk that is sheltered by the garage roof. This is a delightful way to enter this one-story, three-bedroom ranch home. The combination family room-kitchen has sliding glass doors leading to a paved patio, allowing pleasant outdoor dining. Exposed wood-beam cathedral ceilings are featured in this area and extend into the living-dining area.

If you are looking for a Spanish or hacienda-inspired design that will fit in with other styles in your neighborhood, this plan could be the answer.

TOTAL LIVING AREA: Floor area   1,550 sq. ft.
                      Arcade and garage   630 sq. ft.

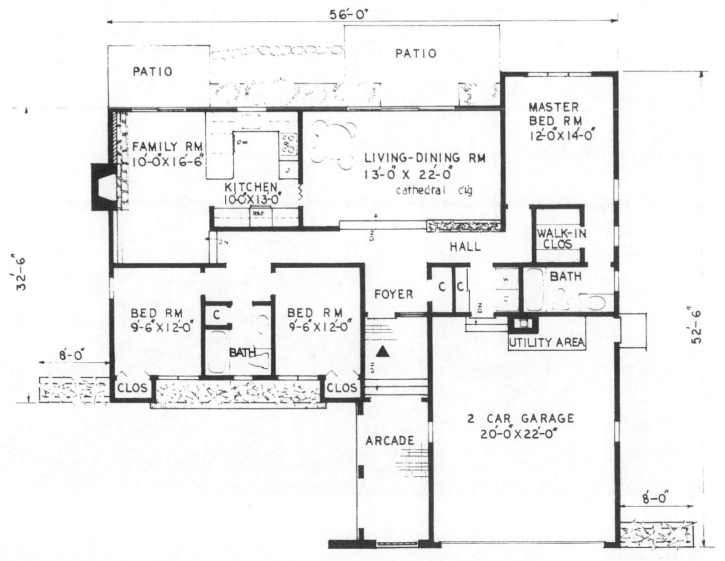

The Grandville

Generous glazing, a hallmark of contemporary styling, and interesting angles softened by the use of fieldstone veneer and vertical redwood siding give this three bedroom ranch a distinctive modern look.

From the entrance foyer you get an impression of roominess, for you can view the living-dining room as well as the family room with the patio beyond the sliding glass doors. Notable features are the dramatic corner fireplace with wraparound raised flagstone hearth and the sloped beamed ceilings in the living areas which add a sense of spaciousness.

The bedroom area has three bedrooms clustered around a minimum hallway and is clearly delineated for maximum privacy and good sound conditioning with a buffer zone of closets and bathrooms.

For active families whose style is casual, this single story contemporary design is an ideal choice.

TOTAL LIVING AREA: 1485 sq. ft.
Laundry & Garage 625 sq. ft.
Basement 1570 sq. ft.
Patio 225 sq. ft.

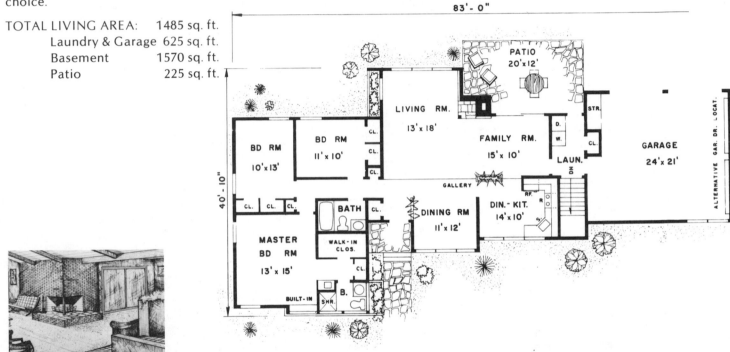

The Landis

Vertically applied natural wood siding emphasizes the contemporary lines of this three-bedroom, one-story home. The floor plan is designed for the informal living preferred by many families.

A sheltered entry leads to the spacious foyer. It is just a few steps to the combination dropped living room/family room and beyond to the wrap-around flagstone patio.

The bedroom wing is isolated from the center of activity and is well arranged as a convenient unit. The master bedroom has three closets and a full bath with shower.

If convenient living is of primary importance in your search for a new home, this modern, ranch-style design could be your best choice.

TOTAL LIVING AREA: First floor   1,468 sq. ft.
                     Basement   790 sq. ft.
                     Garage and laundry   622 sq. ft.

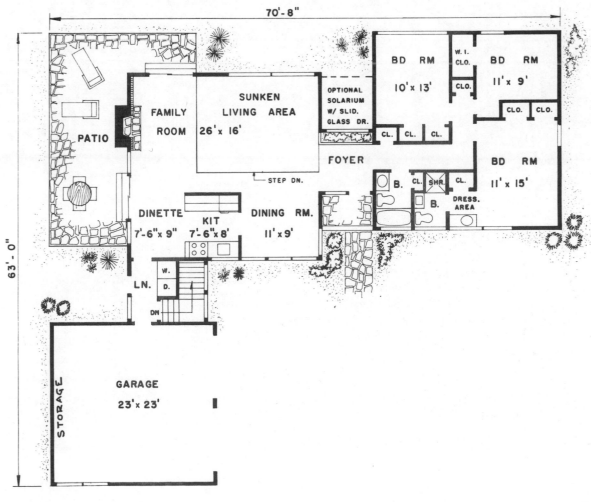

The Edwards

From the picturesque shutters and planting box gracing the front to the breezy rear terrace with its useful barbecue pit for those summer get-togethers, this popular design has answered the dreams of many.

There are three large bedrooms conveniently located near the two full baths and more closet space than you will ever be able to fill. The spacious living-dining room and modern kitchen with its cozy dinette have won wide acclaim.

Completing this wonderful ranch home, the basement level contains a large laundry room with adjoining bath.

TOTAL LIVING AREA: 1,644 sq. ft.

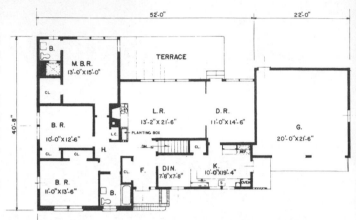

The Fleetwood

The amount of living space in this home is remarkable considering its compact design. A full complement of elements here are usually found in much larger homes. This home also has a hobby room to keep anyone close to the family while pursuing special interests. The two baths, family room, large kitchen and three bedrooms make this truly a family home.

TOTAL LIVING AREA: 1,658 sq. ft. excluding garage

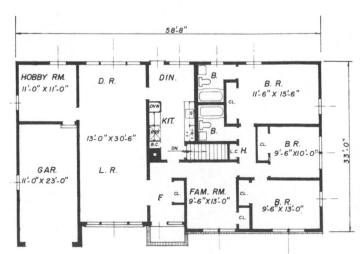

The Marlowe

Here is the complete home you have been looking for, all on one floor.

Entrance to its two car garage may be from any of three sides, depending on your lot size. Upon entering, directly ahead is the living room and dining room with its handsome common window wall and built-in glass china cabinet in the dining room.

From the kitchen with its separate table area, you enter the room of many uses. This family room, opening directly to a covered patio, provides for indoor, outdoor living and entertaining.

In the foyer there is an eye catching brick planter and grilled wall at the living room, which gives this area a very handsome look.

The main bath, with its convenient location, also serves as a guest powder room.

Three spacious bedrooms, including abundant closet space and private bath with stall shower for the master bedroom, will satisfy the family's needs.

TOTAL LIVING AREA: Living area   1,675 sq. ft.
                        Garage   535 sq. ft.

The Fairhaven

One of the better modern trends is placing the living room at the rear of a house. This plan features a sweeping 28 foot 6 inch combined living and dining area overlooking a large back terrace. When a home-owner plans a garden for beauty, it is usually placed in the back yard. There is no better place to view the results of this garden planning than from the living room through the brilliant expanse of unobstructed glass provided in this superlatively designed room. This plan also features an unusually roomy kitchen, in the front, naturally close to the main entrance but with a service entrance at the garage side.

The bedrooms are located off the main hall in a well separated, private wing. The arrangement is a good one, providing cross ventilation for all bedrooms. There is lots of closet space. The two bathrooms, one a private shower room for the master bedroom, are located back-to-back for economy. This plan offers a practical and efficient arrangement of rooms to fill the needs of the family that appreciates a truly fine home.

TOTAL LIVING AREA: 1,604 sq. ft.

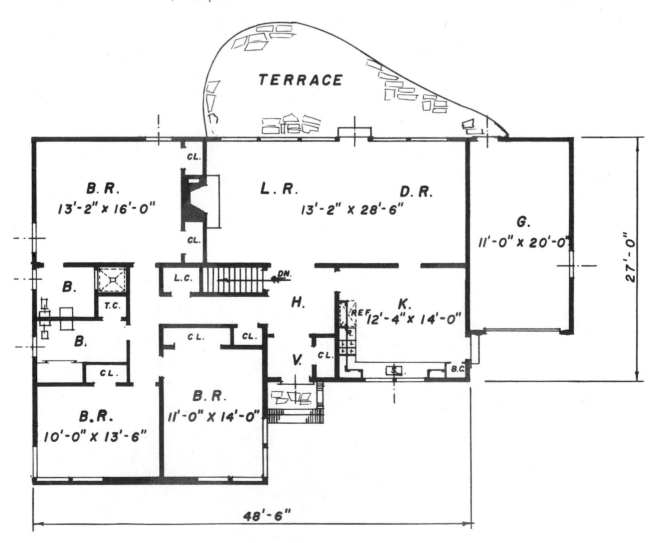

The Fordham

Here is the ranch with a very modern look. The plan is L-shape, compact and ideal for most lots and budgets. It has three large bedrooms, all with oversized closets. The two full baths will satisfy the requirements of most families.

The entertainment center of this home is accessible from the foyer, which also provides a continuous flow of traffic between living, dining and family rooms. A cathedral ceiling with exposed beams is a feature of the living and dining room of this design. This area also has a floor-to-ceiling window wall. The doors may be located at either the front or the back of the garage as required by the position of the house on the site.

TOTAL LIVING AREA: 1,680 sq. ft. excluding porch and garage

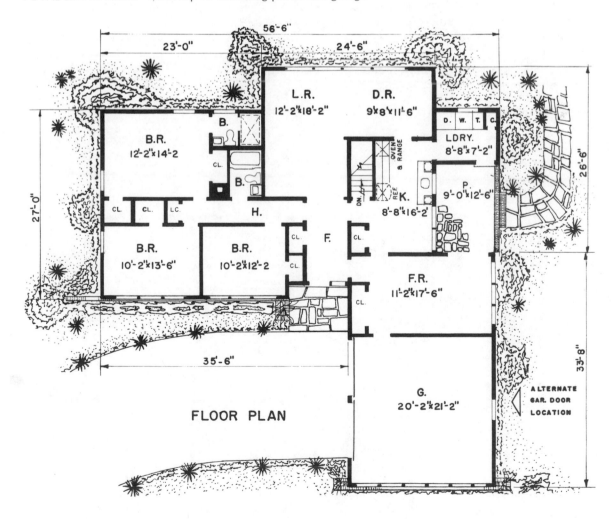

FLOOR PLAN

The Stratton

All the comforts of one-level living are found in this rambling ranch house. From the convenient foyer and halls to the spacious garage, here is a house you will be thrilled to call your home.

The peaceful sleeping area, separated from the rest of the house, offers complete privacy for its three leisurely bedrooms and two full baths.

You will be impressed with the magnificent, spacious living area which includes a cheerful living room, a delightful dining room, and a perfectly arranged kitchen.

As an added extra, for those bad weather spells, there is a handy door leading from Dad's den to the family garage.

Numerous closets and windows, and a beautiful porch for those summer days add the final touches to this home designed just for you.

TOTAL LIVING AREA: 1,675 sq. ft.

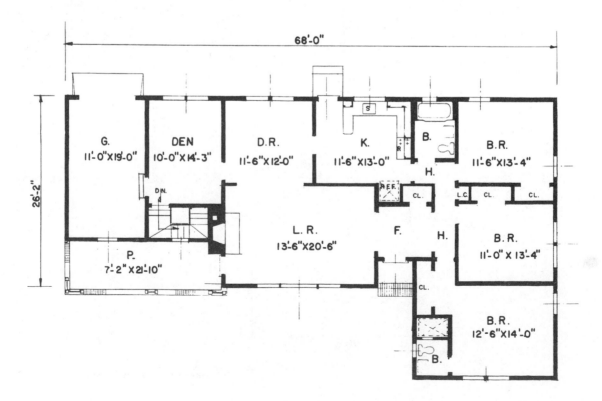

The Ashwood

This two-bedroom contemporary house has a passive solar design to attract and control heat without mechanical assistance. If properly oriented, which means that the house faces north, then the master bedroom, living and dining rooms will be at the south. These rooms have large exposed areas of glass oriented to the low, warming rays of the winter sun. A roof overhang protects these rooms from high summer rays. There are smaller windows on the entrance side, which is further protected from the chill of winter wind by the two-car garage. The sunken living room features a cathedral ceiling and a two-face fireplace with a heat-circulating design.

TOTAL LIVING AREA: First floor   1,628 sq. ft.
                    Laundry room   57 sq. ft.
                    Garage   473 sq. ft.

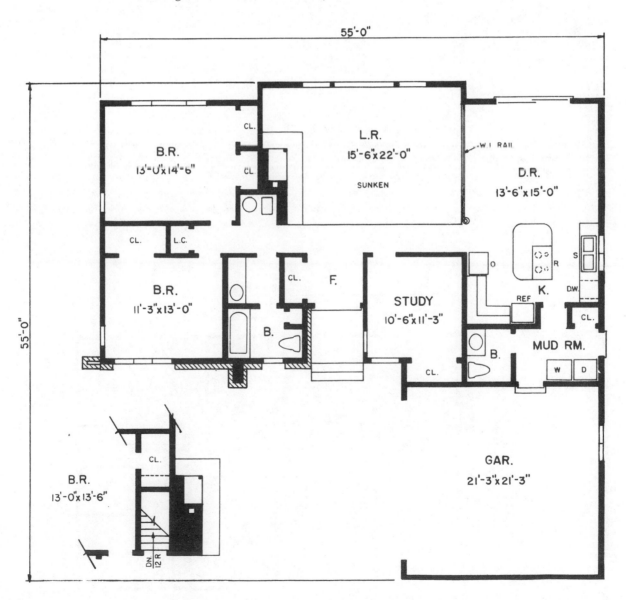

The Charleston

This smart ranch will be a bright and welcoming home. The foyer is nearly large enough to be a reception room, and it has a large coat closet. The area is lighted by a narrow, floor-to-ceiling window. The handsome living-dining L is bright with natural light from three picture windows. The kitchen is a real step-saver, but there is plenty of counter space and cabinets. The living room and bedrooms all have two exposures. The front bedrooms have corner windows that enhance the appearance of the front of the house. The large bath is the family bath; the master bath is totally private. Storage problems are solved because there are eight huge closets in the plan. This attractive house would be an ornament to any neighborhood.

TOTAL LIVING AREA: 1,686 sq. ft.

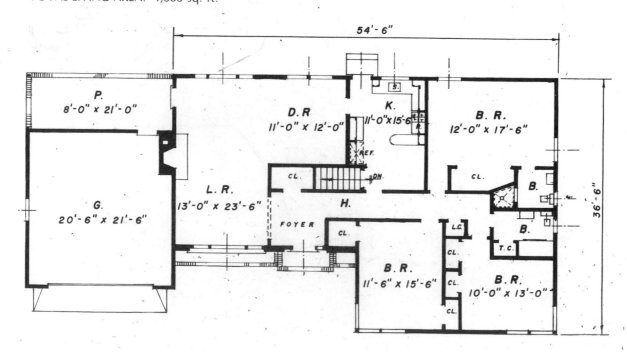

The Madrid

The walled entry and stucco exterior of this three-bedroom, one-story design are unmistakably Spanish.

Inside, sloped, beamed ceilings in the living room, dining and family rooms allow these spaces to appear larger than their actual sizes. The focal point is the sunken conversation area that features a bar and a circular firepit with a cone-shaped, ceiling-suspended hood. Immediate access is available to the rear yard and patio through sliding glass doors.

TOTAL LIVING AREA: Living area   1,592 sq. ft.
                     Laundry   92 sq. ft.
                     Garage   588 sq. ft.

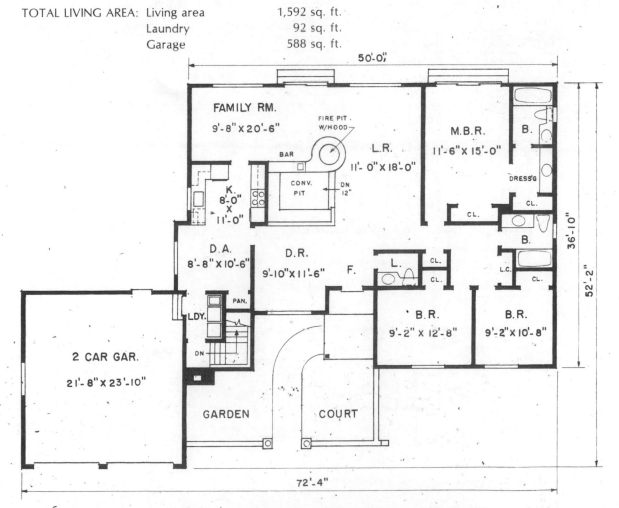

The Wildwood

An enduring quality is presented in the long, low, rangy lines of this ranch home. The entrance is in the shielded corner of the front patio, and inside a smart foyer separates the three-bedroom wing from the living and entertaining areas. And what a living room there is—almost a 25' sweep to the fireplace, and another 25' expanse through the arch of the dining room, from picture window to picture window. Next to the dining room there's an extra, all-purpose room, with two sun-filled window walls. It's convenient from house and garage, and can double as a playroom, study or tremendous television den. Closet walls add spacious storage to the bedrooms, and the family bathroom, economically back-to-back with kitchen plumbing, is supplemented by the master shower-lavatory. The kitchen has a spacious, charming area for dining, as well as cooking in this interesting luxury house.

TOTAL LIVING AREA: 1,710 sq. ft. (excl. garage)

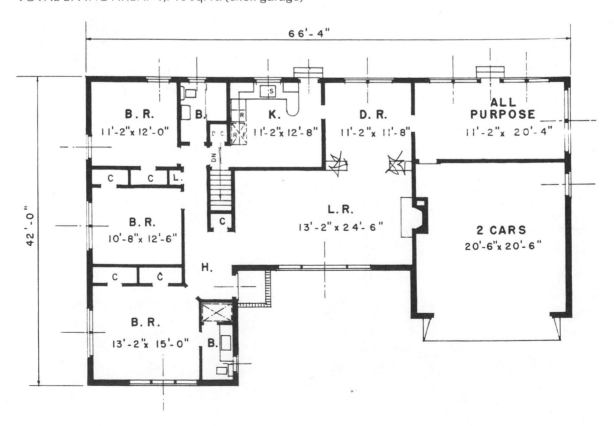

The Whitestone

Being two-faced in this case is not a detriment, quite the contrary as a matter of fact. This "L" shaped ranch home can be set on your lot to present either of two faces to the front, (whichever pleases your individual taste). All rooms are good size and closets are many and large. The living and dining areas combined into an "L" shape make each appear much larger than they really are, and the long kitchen provides ample space for convenient work and breakfast areas. The den is located in such a position that it can serve well as an extra guest room, being directly across the hall from the extra shower-bath-lavatory located next to the kitchen

TOTAL LIVING AREA: 1,715 sq. ft.

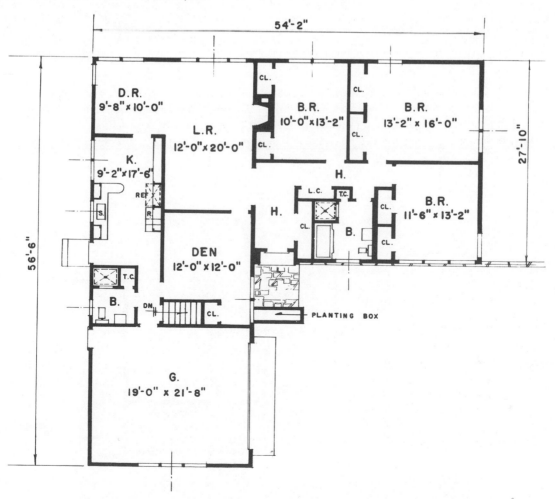

The Knowles

A dove cote, wood shingles and vertical board siding have been skillfully blended to create an eye-appealing exterior that complements the well planned interior of this ranch home. Each room in the design has been scaled to contribute the maximum potential to pleasant living. A few of the features that make this ranch design the favorite of many are centralized plumbing, generous closet space, and ample window areas.

TOTAL LIVING AREA: 1,700 sq. ft.

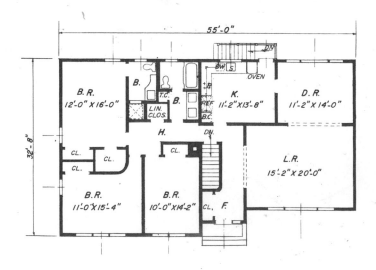

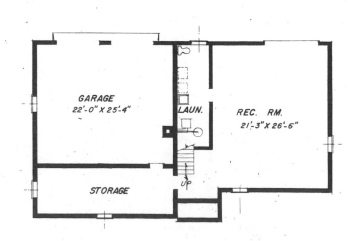

The Talmadge

This ranch design captures the traditional look of classic French styling. A central entrance foyer assures good circulation of traffic in three directions: to the dining room, to the three bedrooms on the left and to the sunken living room that is separated from the foyer by a decorative wrought iron railing. A cathedral ceiling is found in the kitchen-family room, where the family is likely to spend most of its leisure time near the massive brick fireplace.

If you want a spacious and convenient home, this traditional three-bedroom design has all the ingredients of a much larger home and will fit into any setting.

TOTAL LIVING AREA: Living area   1,645 sq. ft.
                    Laundry   105 sq. ft.
                    Garage   522 sq. ft.

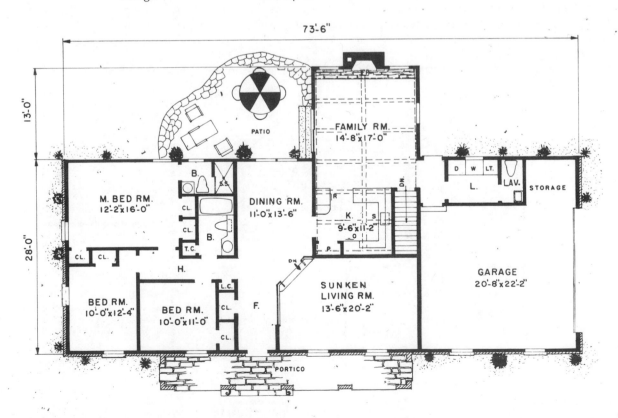

The Malverne

This beautiful ranch house plan has been created for those who enjoy the best in modern living. The plan is logically and efficiently laid out. All the rooms are large. The three bedrooms are extra-sized and have convenient, large closets. The house will be economical to construct because consideration has been given to such things as arranging back-to-back plumbing for the bathrooms.

The roomy kitchen with its dining area is ideal for all informal meals. There is a sunny dining room for more formal occasions. For family living, the comfortable living and dining areas are perfect.

TOTAL LIVING AREA: 1,750 sq. ft.

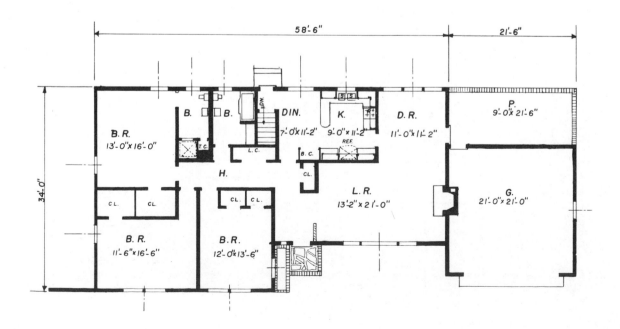

The Lucerne

The ranch plan shown here has been designed for a family that wants a home adapted to informal living. The large activity room located across the rear of the house, directly adjacent to the kitchen and front entrance hall, provides the ideal area for casual recreation and entertaining. There is convenient access to the basement and the garage at the kitchen service entrance. The house contains three bedrooms that are buffered from the noise of activity by closets. The master bedroom has a private bath with a shower.

TOTAL LIVING AREA: 1,757 sq. ft. excluding the garage

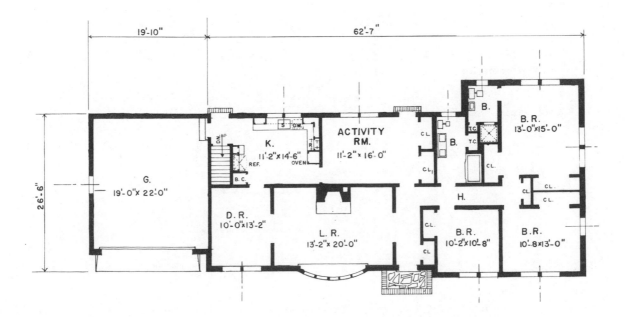

The Lexington

The flavor of old New England is present in the lines of this ranch home for today's living.

Notice that the kitchen is in the front of the house. This location provides many advantages both economical and convenient. All plumbing is at the front of the house, meaning shorter runs to street connections. Circulation within the house is ideal, for the kitchen is directly adjacent to the dining room, porch, exterior and entrance foyer; connecting to all these areas without using other rooms as passageways.

Dining room and living room in the rear provides privacy and a controlled view of your own property area.

Three bedrooms and two baths complete the living area of this home, but there is more — in addition to a full 2 car garage located in the basement, we also find a wonderful recreation room, laundry area and a lavatory, in addition to tremendous area for the heating unit and much storage and work shop area.

An alternate arrangement on the blueprints shows the garage at the front of the house and the recreation room at the rear.

AREA: First floor   1,793 sq. ft. (excl. porch)

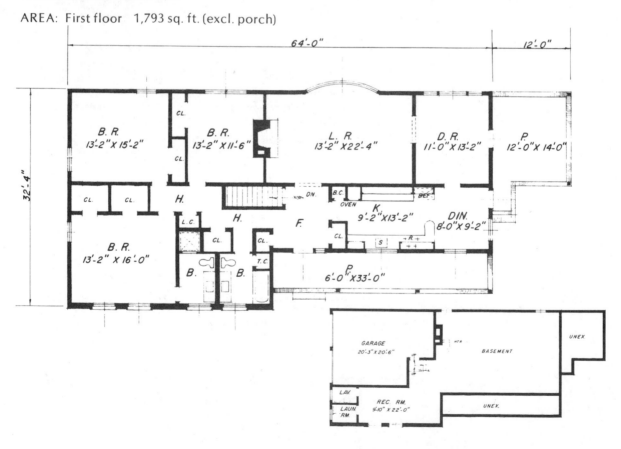

BASEMENT & GARAGE PLAN

The Frontenac

Luxurious living in the contemporary manner is provided in the ultimate in this distinctive one story, three bedroom "rambling" ranch design. Despite its somewhat expansive appearance, it actually is a compact plan with 1,814 square feet of area with eye catching features of the exterior such as vertical stone piers between the living room picture plate glass windows, natural rich color red-wood vertical siding, stone veneer, low hipped roof and the stone planter at the covered entrance portico.

With simplicity as its theme, it fulfills the aim of producing a design with plenty of exterior sparkle.

TOTAL LIVING AREA: 1,814 sq. ft.
    Basement   888 sq. ft.
    Garage   529 sq. ft.

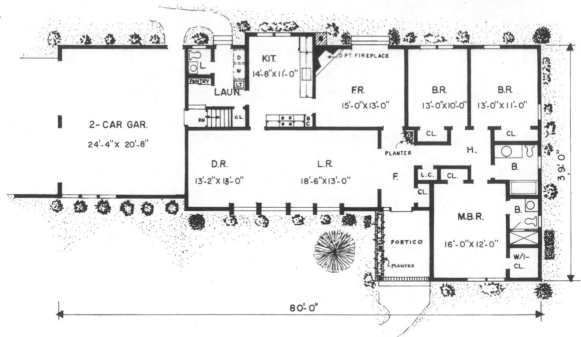

The Riverdale

Here is a ranch house that specializes in living conveniences. Some of the many features which afford these conveniences are the walk-in closets with plenty of space—no crowding of clothes ever—and a long sliding-door linen closet with many shelves providing all the storage space you will ever need. There is a separate vanity in the main bath, a large vanitory in the master bath and three very large bedrooms. Notice the small alcove off the kitchen leading from outside directly down to the basement. The living and dining rooms form a spacious bright and airy "ell" with views front and rear through large window areas. As a final touch there is an ample sized two car garage attached. It is accessible through the long open porch area directly off the dining room.

TOTAL LIVING AREA: 1,860 sq. ft.

The Farmstead

Here is a rambling ranch house with four bedrooms, laundry and family rooms plus 2½ baths, all in less than 1,900 sq. ft.

Wood shingles, combined with board and batten exterior siding along with a graceful entrance portico give this home an eye appeal that will be hard to beat.

Adjoining the kitchen, the paneled family room with colonial fireplace, and glass sliding doors, allows for ideal "outside-inside" living.

The kitchen with separate dinette, adjoining the laundry, lavatory and two car garage make for ideal traffic circulation.

All bedrooms have oversized closets, excellent wall space and more than adequate natural light and ventilation.

After studying this plan, one will have to agree that its design is sure to be a leader in any community.

TOTAL LIVING AREA: 1,898 sq. ft.

The Curran

Modern living in the atmosphere of the old colonial is found in this popular design.

Four spacious bedrooms with ample closet space are conveniently located to bring you the seclusion and privacy you desire.

A built-in two-car garage is found in the basement.

TOTAL LIVING AREA: 1,885 sq. ft.

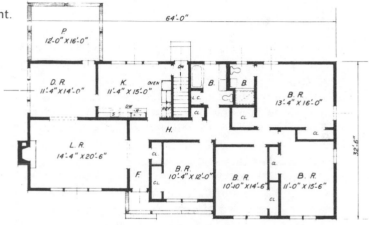

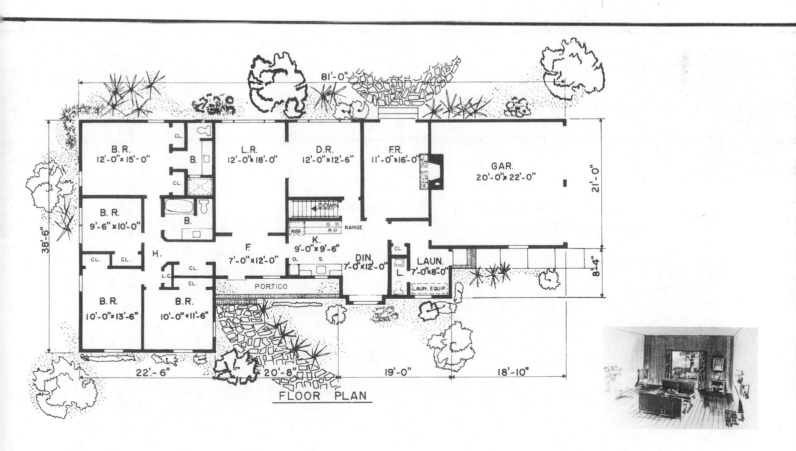

FLOOR PLAN

The Bayshore

This hip roof ranch has an exterior that tastefully blends walls of brick and wood shingles.

The entrance foyer is centrally located between the living-dining areas and the sleeping quarters.

The family room, kitchen and laundry room are in line in the back part of the house. Fully equipped with modern appliances and plenty of counter and storage space, the kitchen has a dinette area which looks out to the rear garden and patio. To the left of the kitchen is the laundry room with pantry and adjacent lavatory. There are doors in the laundry leading to the rear yard and to the two-car garage.

To the right of the foyer is a hall leading to three bedrooms and two baths. The two front bedrooms will accommodate most furniture arrangements. The master bedroom, also with excellent wall space, has two closets and its own bath, the latter tiled, with its basin set in an attractive, built-in vanitory, and with a stall shower.

This ranch house is sure to be a leader in any community.

TOTAL LIVING AREA: 1,830 sq. ft.

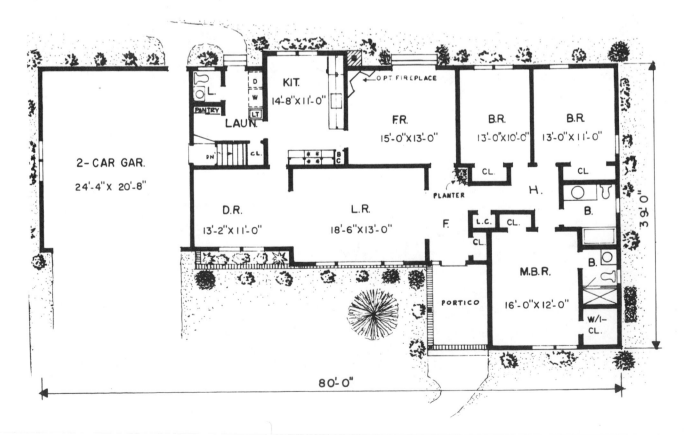

The Lewiston

A refreshing exterior is boasted by this popular ranch design which will make it a hit in any neighborhood.

Including three airy bedrooms, a modern kitchen and the combination sunken living-dining room.

Gable roofs and shingles highlight the exterior of this roomy ranch home.

Inside we see a well designed layout featuring large rooms each conveniently located. A library is also provided which, if needed, may serve as another bedroom. Two full baths back-to-back make for plumbing economy.

These and many other features make this a popular home.

TOTAL LIVING AREA: 1,900 sq. ft.

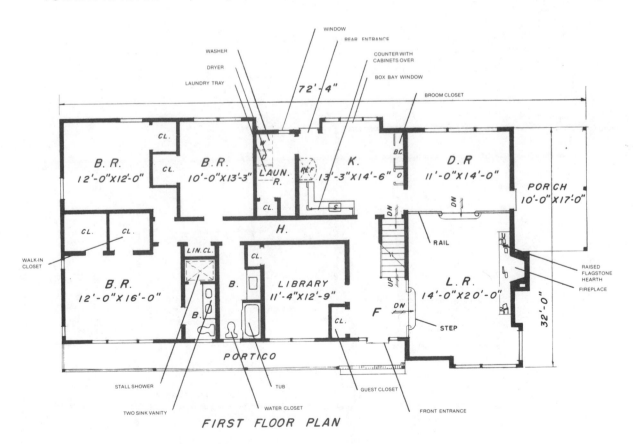

FIRST FLOOR PLAN

The Eldorado

This delightful design presents a contemporary exterior to complement its beautiful spacious interior.

Every possible convenience to make living comfortable has been included on one floor, and the need for a basement has been eliminated. Easy access has been provided from the living room and the kitchen to the patio in keeping with the modern trend for outdoor living.

TOTAL LIVING AREA: 1,880 sq. ft.

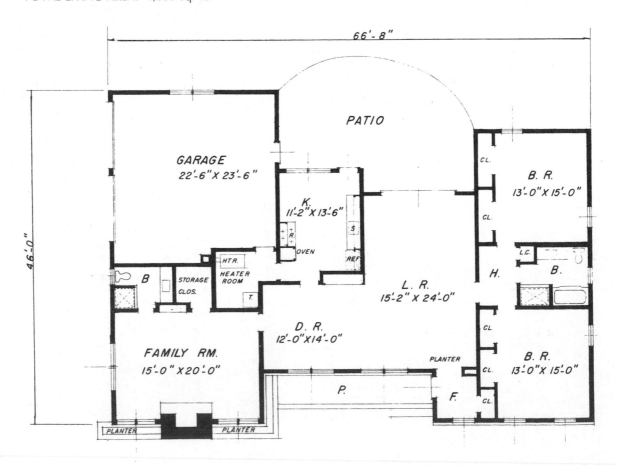

The Dunbar

Condensed in this compact ranch home, formed in the popular "L" shape, are all the features found in many larger and more expensive homes. It has tremendous closet space, conveniently located throughout the entire house, three ample sized bedrooms, with a spacious family room off the kitchen. Leaded glass windows give this home the typical spreading look of a colonial

TOTAL LIVING AREA: 1,945 sq. ft.

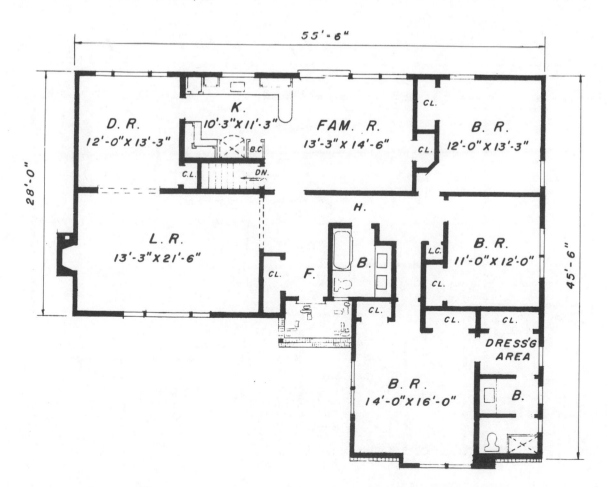

The Baxter

Beauty and simplicity, together with thoughts of economy, have been united to create this three bedroom stone veneer and wood shingle design. The unusual cozy layout has all the privacy of a two story house with the sleeping area separated from the living activity.

The large living room and dining room give a spaciousness usually found only in much larger and expensive homes. A two car garage is conveniently located under the bedroom area.

Dress up the planting box at the entrance with your favorite flowers, and this house will stand out among others with your own personal touch.

TOTAL LIVING AREA: 2,125 sq. ft.

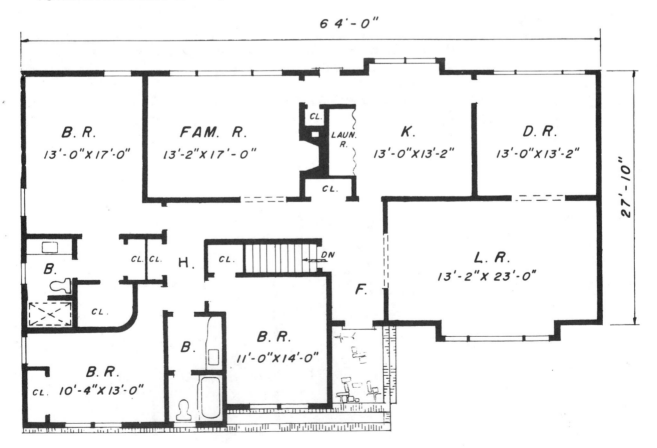

The Sturbridge

Entering beneath the covered portico into a larger foyer, one moves straight ahead to the living room, to the left and the four-bedroom wing, or to the right and the kitchen. This distributes traffic effectively.

The living room has plenty of wall areas suited for varieties of furniture arrangements, but the feature is the fireplace wall. It's made of floor-to-ceiling brick throughout its length, with an oversized, extended flagstone hearth. The back of the fireplace gives the dining room an interesting bricked projection. Next to the dining room is a wood-paneled family room, with full-height sliding glass doors leading to a rear patio.

Headquarters for housekeeping is in front of the home in an efficient kitchen that includes a countertop range, a wall oven and a separate breakfast area. Also in this area is the service entry, with a mud-room closet, lavatory and laundry that contains a washer, dryer and storage cabinet facilities.

The four-bedroom, two-bath wing has a hall flared out at the end to eliminate a feeling of congestion. All bedrooms have an abundance of closet space, with three others in the hall. The master bedroom has a full bath, including a stall shower, an oversize vanity with full-length wall mirror and separated, water-closet compartment.

TOTAL LIVING AREA: First floor   2,134 sq. ft.

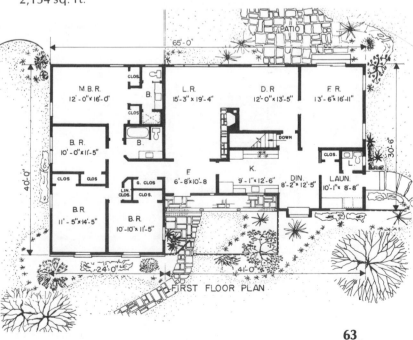

FIRST FLOOR PLAN

The Pearson

This homey design will form a perfect picture of beauty in any neighborhood.

The basement contains a roomy two car garage and ample room for a future recreation room.

A convenient lavatory is found off the kitchen and foyer. The dining area is highlighted by a picturesque box bay.

TOTAL LIVING AREA: 1,950 sq. ft.

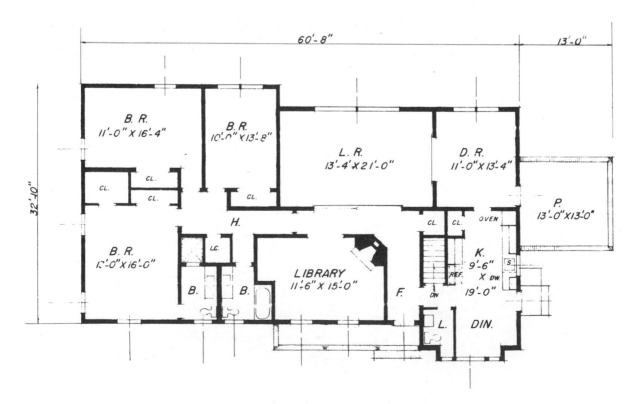

The Lamont

Four large bedrooms, two full baths and many convenient closets form the discrete and serene sleeping area.

Convenience and spaciousness keynote the rest of the house. Living room with fireplace, a large cheery kitchen with dining alcove and dining room access to patio enjoyment complete the design for gracious one level living.

TOTAL LIVING AREA: 1,955 sq. ft.

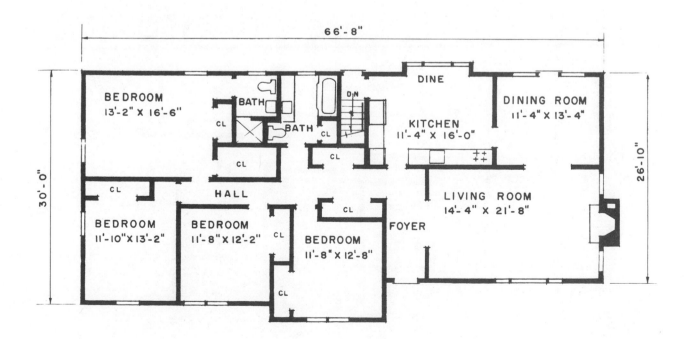

The Dorian

This three bedroom ranch home is designed for informal living, but it has, too, all the regal arrangements of the formal home. A through hall entrance, leading directly to the kitchen area and separating living and sleeping areas, provides all the dignity and grace of well-planned circulation. Two full size baths and lots of extra separate closet space for clothes, linen and towels, plus three bedrooms, all with ample room for twin or double size beds and furniture, complete this home—designed for the finest living in the most pleasing manner.

TOTAL LIVING AREA: 1,945 sq. ft.

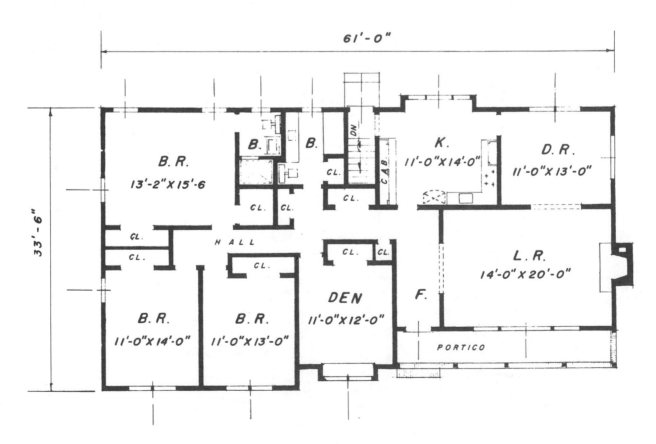

The Clarke

This contemporary styled ranch plan offers many desirable features for today's living.

The large utilities room on the living level with convenient lavatory provides direct access to kitchen, outdoors and basement.

The open "L" shape of living-dining rooms and the spaciousness of the entrance foyer accent the free feeling of modern uncluttered living.

TOTAL LIVING AREA: 1,985 sq. ft.
(excluding porch & garage)

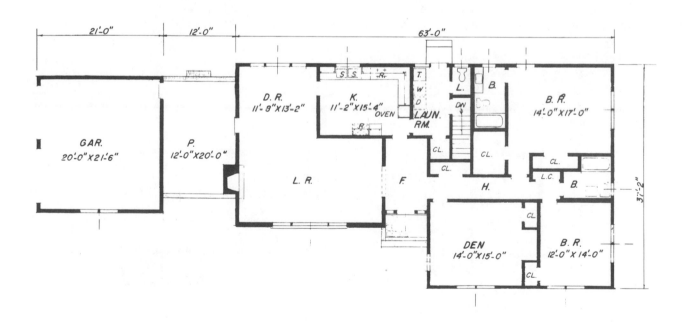

The Scottsdale

A transverse gabled roof runs from the front to the rear of this contemporary design, sheltering the front entry and creating a dramatic cathedral ceiling in the living room. Situated at the center of the house, the main entrance and sunken living-entertaining area acts as a buffer between the kitchen and the dining room on one side, and the sleeping quarters on the right.

Sliding doors in the living-room, the dining room, and the dinette, open onto a spacious wrap-around wood deck. An ornamental stairway leads down from the entrance foyer to an area designed for social gatherings, recreation, and family activities, and to the garage. The plan also includes two family bedrooms with plenty of closet space, and a master bedroom suite with a private bath.

TOTAL LIVING AREA: First Floor   1,980 sq. ft.
                   Garage   750 sq. ft.

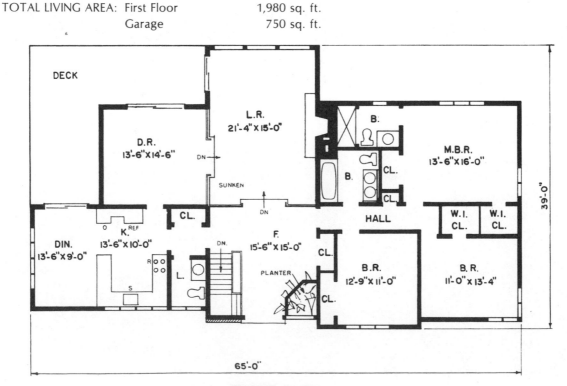

FLOOR PLAN

The Glennon

This three-bedroom, two-bath ranch home incorporates the increasingly popular arrangement of living and dining rooms at the rear. Combining the best features of the conventional and the new in modern living, this plan surpasses most other modern plans for economy and convenience of living. Entry is through the front foyer or directly from the garage.

TOTAL LIVING AREA: 2,000 sq. ft.

FIRST FLOOR PLAN

50'-6"

71'-0"

B. R.
12'-0"X 15'-0"

B.

B. R.
11'-0"X13'-0"

CL.

CL.

L.R.   D.R.
13'-0" X 30'-0"

CL.   CL

DN

DIN.

L.C

B. R.
11'-0"X 15'-0"

DEN
12'-0"X15'-0"

11'-0"X 19'-0"

CL.

B.

F.

K.

DN

CL.

GARAGE
21'-0" X 22'-0"

The Graham

This large ranch plan draws on colonial influences for its exterior styling. The finish combines brick, wood shingles and flush board siding. A dove cote and a planter are the exterior decorative highlights.

The interior plan allows a smooth flow of traffic but efficiently separates the sleeping, formal entertaining and family recreation areas. There are many extra features, such as large closets and a built-in china cabinet, that contribute to pleasant and comfortable living in this home.

TOTAL LIVING AREA: 2,010 sq. ft.

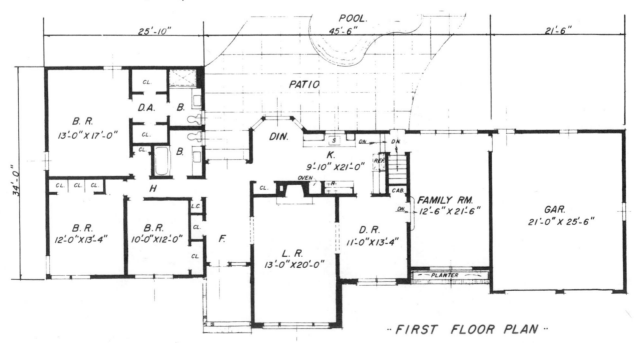

·· FIRST FLOOR PLAN ··

The Kendall

This contemporary ranch has been planned as an answer to building on a sloping lot. There are indoor and outdoor living areas on both the first and the basement levels. One level has been designed primarily for the adults and one for the children in the family.

   All the rooms are spacious and offer adequate area for family activities. The front bedroom may be divided into two rooms if necessary for extra sleeping space or to provide a separate playroom.

TOTAL LIVING AREA: 2,115 sq. ft.

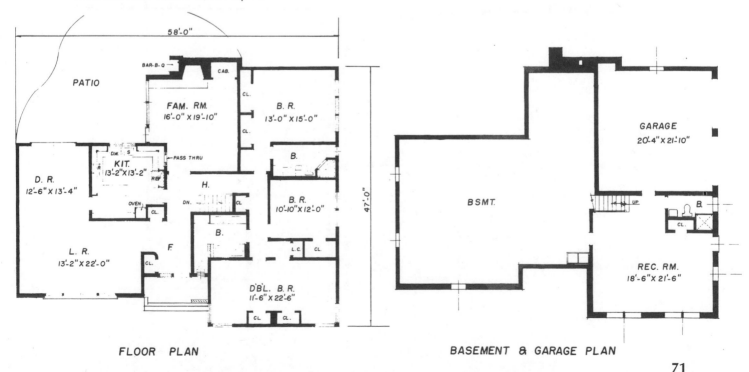

FLOOR PLAN   BASEMENT & GARAGE PLAN

The Riviera

In these days of high building costs, it is nice to know that you need not spend a fortune to achieve comfort and the look of luxury.

The first impressive sight of the interior of this home is gained upon entering the front foyer. The view is of the enormous, 21 by 24 foot Great Room, which has a massive fireplace and an all-glass rear wall.

Although the house can be built on a fairly level lot, the oversize, two-car garage is designed to be built under the bedroom wing. However, the garage can be built onto the kitchen-dinette if your lot is flat.

TOTAL LIVING AREA: First floor   2,124 sq. ft.
                           Garage   700 sq. ft.
                           Basement   1,424 sq. ft.

68'-0"

39'-0"

DECK

GREAT RM.
21'-3" x 24'-3"

D.R.
13'-6" x 15'-6"

DN.

S.S.

B.

M.B.R.
13'-6" x 16'-0"

CL.

B.

L.C.

CL.

O.

REF.

DIN.
9'-0" x 13'-6"

K.
10'-0" x 13'-6"

CL.

H.

W.I.
CL.

W.I.
CL.

DN.

DN.

R.

L.

S.

F.
15'-0" x 15'-6"

PLANTER

CL.

CL.

B.R.
11'-0" x 12'-9"

B.R.
11'-0" x 13'-3"

FLOOR PLAN

The Hacienda

While the exterior architectural details of this three bedroom one-story house adhere to the Spanish motif, the floor plan is arranged for present-day living.

The entrance is most impressive with wrought iron gates leading to the front door through a private, typical "ranchero" treatment.

This house is for the family that wants the conveniences of today wrapped in a look of yesterday.

TOTAL LIVING AREA: 2,145 sq. ft.

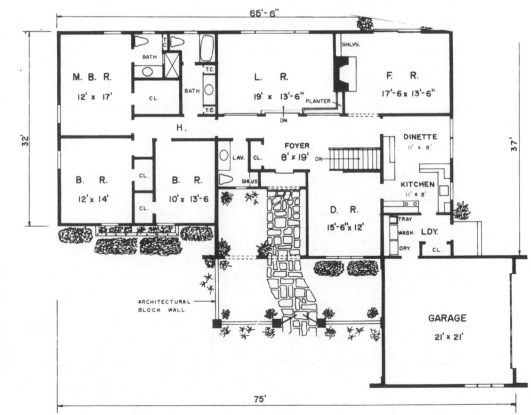

The Blaine

Here is an exclusive ranch design featuring a circular foyer. A handy powder room and a large living room are only a few of the features to be found in this contemporary design.

The bedroom area contains three large bedrooms, two baths, and ample closet space. Here we also find a cozy den for Dad. A large kitchen and dining room open out to the terrace with its handy barbecue pit.

TOTAL LIVING AREA: 2,145 sq. ft.

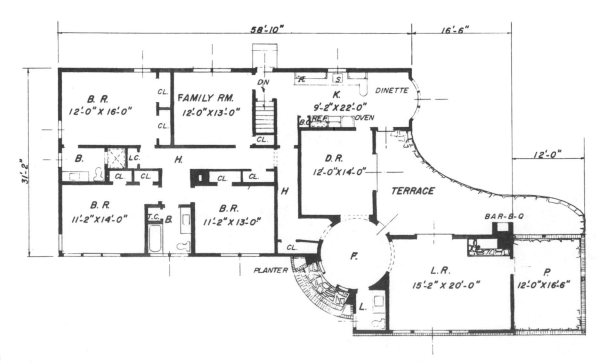

The Regent

Gable roofs, stone veneer and a modern retaining wall form a beautiful exterior to accent this captivating ranch design.

The floor plan reveals back-to-back plumbing, a cozy fireplace in the den, and numerous closets and sunny windows.

A built in two car garage is to be found in the basement layout along with ample space for a future recreation room.

TOTAL LIVING AREA: 2,145 sq. ft.

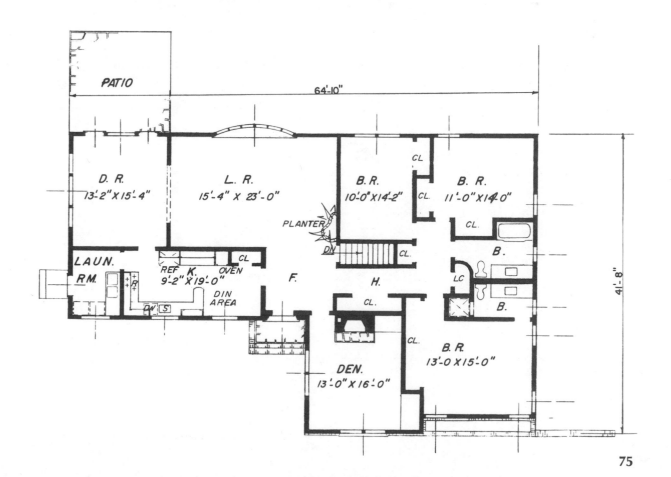

The Pickford

Here is a compact, modern ranch that is ideal for many lots and budgets. The home has three large bedrooms with oversized closets and two and one-half baths, meeting the needs of most families. The entertainment center of the home is accessible from the foyer, which allows a continuous flow to the living, dining and family rooms. The living and family rooms are out of the traffic pattern, so no one need pass through either to reach another room. Garage doors may be located on any of the exposed sides for most convenient access.

TOTAL LIVING AREA: 2,180 sq. ft.

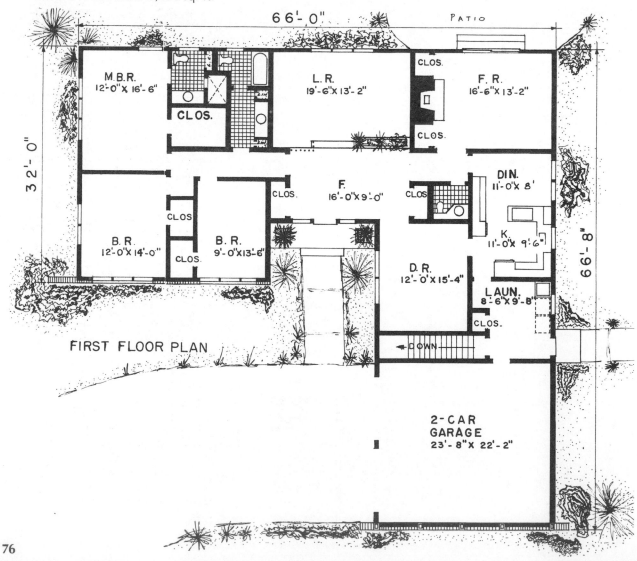

FIRST FLOOR PLAN

The Sandlewood

Here is a plan designed for those who prefer to avoid the extremes of either the contemporary or the traditional. The entrance roof, vertical windows and cathedral ceiling in the foyer bring exterior and interior interest together in this three-bedroom ranch. The sleeping wing has a master bedroom with two walk-in closets, a vanity, a dressing room and a private bath. A full bath services the other bedrooms.

TOTAL LIVING AREA: Living area   2,510 sq. ft.
                  Garage   550 sq. ft.

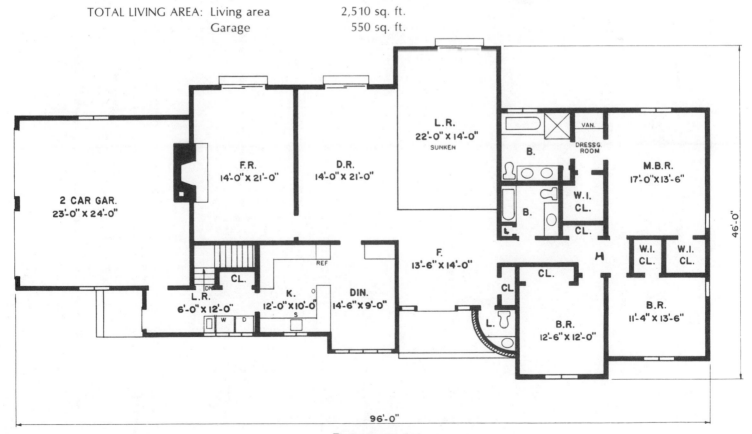

FLOOR PLAN

The Villanova

This latest design with that increasingly popular Spanish-Colonial influence makes you feel like a nobleman of a past era with all the advantages of modern materials and conveniences.

Accentuated by the low-walled wrought-iron and main entrance gates, rough stucco finish, projecting stained wood beams, arched windows, paved courtyard with circular fountain, ceramic tile entrance foyer floor and a screened-in patio large enough to include the optional swimming pool lend an exotic air of a Spanish villa to this design.

Although the plan is basementless, a full or partial basement is possible with the basement stair located where the large utility closet is shown in the laundry area. The laundry is complete with washer, dryer and accessible to the two car garage.

This design, pure or modified, seems perfectly adapted to today's living and has a romance that is typical of the traditionally Spanish-styled homes.

AREA: Living area   2,060 sq. ft.
         Garage   460 sq. ft.
         Screened patio   870 sq. ft.

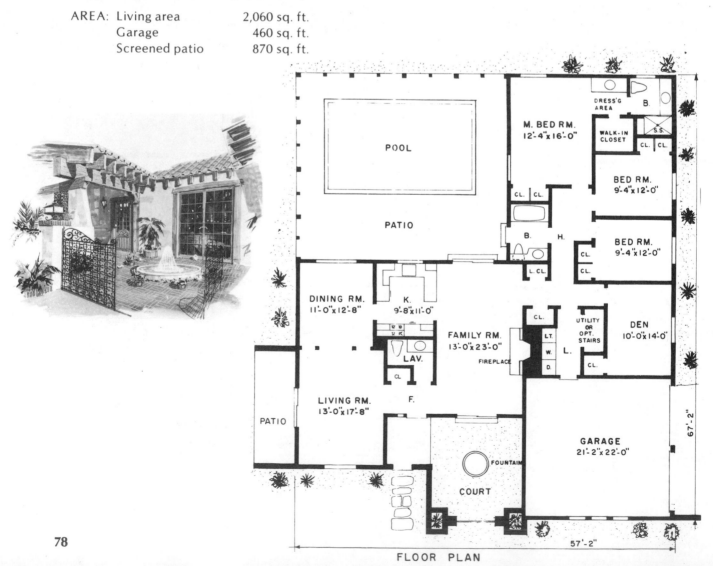

FLOOR PLAN

The Norwood

A ranch house consisting of seven rooms and including a two-car garage and two baths will be your family's favorite.

Three of the rooms are bedrooms. The den might serve as an occasional fourth bedroom when there are extra guests. Ordinarily it is more apt to be a television room and is shaped accordingly—24½′ long. The other rooms include an efficiency U-type kitchen, dining room and an enormous living room 29′ long. There are no less than ten closets, and book cases flank the living room fireplace. In the same rooms two virtually unbroken walls permit attractive placement of large pieces of furniture.

TOTAL LIVING AREA: 2,087 sq. ft. (excluding garage)

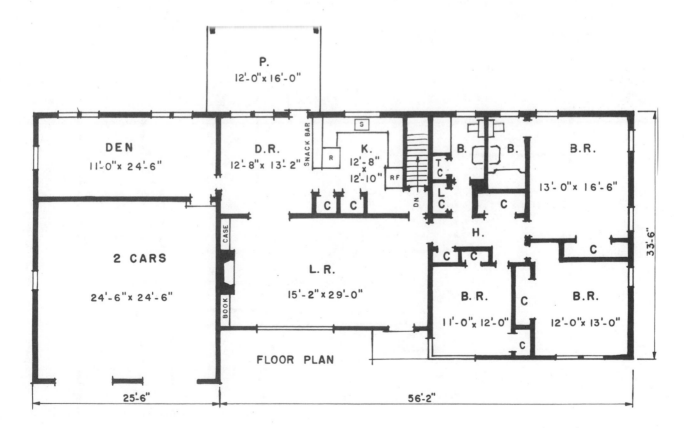

The Thornhill

The twin-gable facade of this contemporary, three-bedroom ranch gives visual interest to the exterior of this home. A centrally located, spacious foyer serves the living room, kitchen, family-room, basement steps and the bedroom wing. Sliding doors give a view of the yard and link the dinette to the natural surroundings.

A massive brick fireplace is the focal point of the beamed-ceiling family room. The bedroom section contains three bedrooms with huge closets. This area is well isolated from the living area. The two full bathrooms are adjacent to each other to minimize the cost of plumbing.

If you like contemporary design but want a home to blend into a neighborhood with other, more traditional styles, this plan deserves serious consideration.

TOTAL LIVING AREA: First floor   2,516 sq. ft.
                     Garage   944 sq. ft.

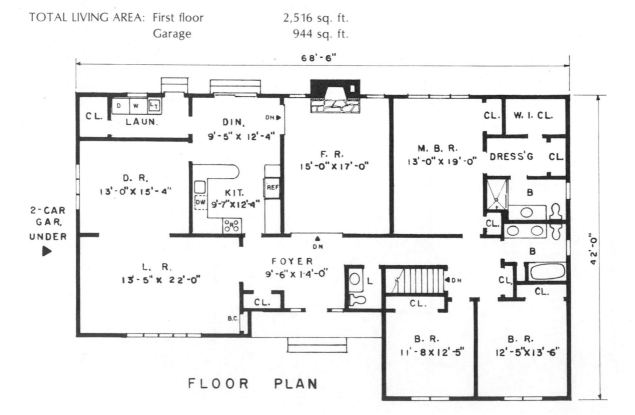

FLOOR PLAN

The Radcliff

An important feature of this three-bedroom, contemporary colonial design is the division between the living and sleeping zones. Straight ahead from the foyer is the sunken living room that is open to but separated from the dining room by a decorative railing. The beamed ceiling of the family room continues into the kitchen-dinette that has a full complement of cabinets and appliances.

The bedrooms are to the right of the foyer. The master suite has a private bath and a room-size, walk-in closet. The other two bedrooms are located near the family bath. Basement stairs are off the garage.

TOTAL LIVING AREA: First floor   2,580 sq. ft.
Garage   480 sq. ft.
Basement   1,767 sq. ft.

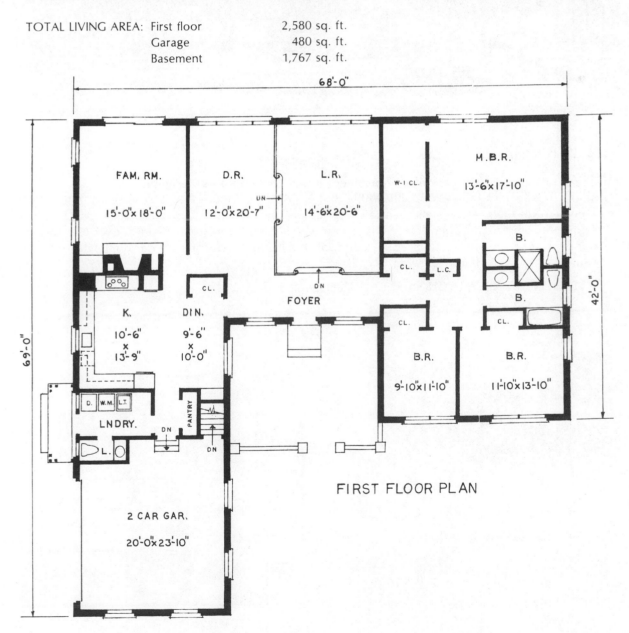

FIRST FLOOR PLAN

The Menlo

Restraint and sophistication are combined in this contemporary design which utilizes vertical siding . . . special windows and interesting roof to produce a house that is different, yet has clean architectural lines. Among the eye-catching features of the exterior of this eight room, three or four bedroom ranch design is a trellised roof which casts interesting shadows over the double-door entrance . . . and the tapered skylight roof which admits natural light during the day into the central foyer of the bedroom wing.

TOTAL LIVING AREA: 2,218 sq. ft. (excluding garage)

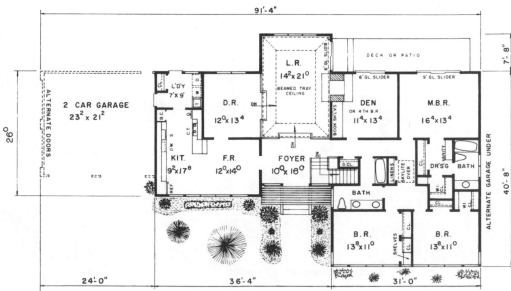

The Rutledge

This "L" shaped ranch design provides comfortable living for all. Additional living area has been provided with the inclusion of a family room and T.V. room.

Many features are included in this design to bring you a home that you can truly be happy to own.

TOTAL LIVING AREA: 2,290 sq. ft. (excl. garage)

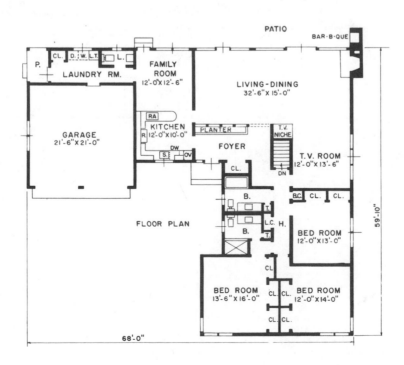

The Covington

Traditional in appearance, with an air of warmth and comfort, this ranch would be an attractive addition to any community.

A covered, long portico leads to the centrally located foyer. Directly to the rear of the foyer is a sunken living room and adjoining dining room with a wrought iron rail acting as a divider.

To the right of the foyer the wood-paneled family room has a brick-faced fireplace that is visible almost immediately after entering the front door.

Between the combined kitchen-dinette and the garage is the laundry room which contains a closet for cleaning supplies and equipment. The laundry room has two doors and one to the garage.

The two rear bedrooms, with the main bathroom between, will accommodate most furniture arrangements. The master bedroom with its dressing area and spacious closets, one of which is a walk-in type, complete this lovely ranch.

TOTAL LIVING AREA: 2,336 sq. ft.

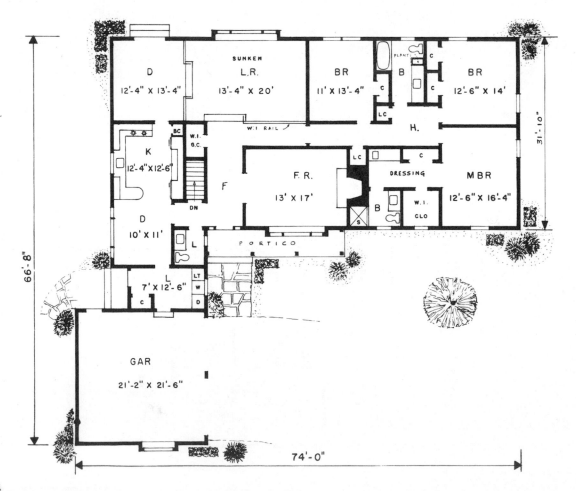

The Fairview

Here is a plan with the new concept for living. Closets galore are situated at the entrance and within the bedroom wing. The kitchen is a dream in work area and separate breakfast alcove. There is a lavatory conveniently located just off the kitchen and readily accessible to the rear entrance which is through the activity room. This room is down a few steps and sports a bright and rugged tile floor This is an ideal room for children's play or party and certainly will be used by parents for less formal entertaining. The roomy 2 car garage is a built-in feature and has access through the house for rainy weather.

TOTAL LIVING AREA: 2,375 sq. ft.

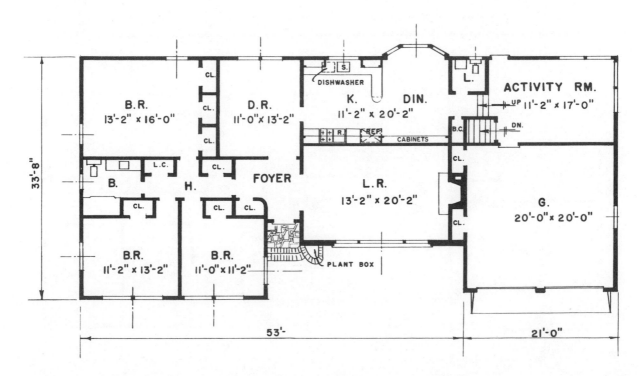

The Hallmark

The comfort and convenience of the ranch style home are unsurpassed. Here is a plan combining all the attributes of up-to-date planning for modern living, yet presenting the formal character of tradition in its outward appearance.

The new trend for outdoor living is accented here by a large sliding glass wall in the den for unrestricted flow between indoors and outdoors.

The master bedroom suite, consisting of dressing alcove, closets and private shower bath, is accompanied by two additional master sized bedrooms and a second full bath, all well supplied with ample closets. A separate lavatory is located convenient to the kitchen, den and living room. The kitchen is arranged for step saving meal preparation, and the breakfast area is located in a bright windowed corner.

A maid's room and bath, laundry room at the service entrance and a spacious 2 car garage finally complete this wonderfully liveable home.

TOTAL LIVING AREA: 2,708 sq. ft.

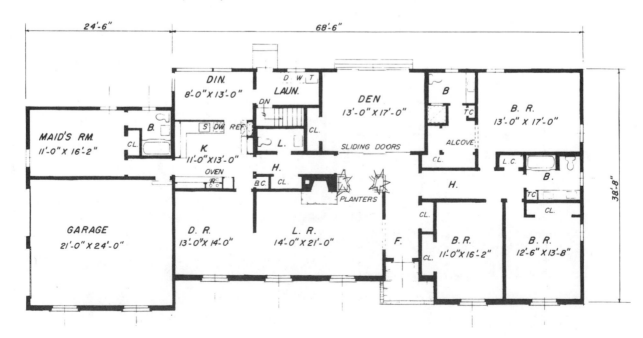

The Lambert

Interesting angles and clerestory windows, softened by the use of fieldstone veneer and redwood vertical siding, give this gentle three bedroom contemporary ranch a distinctive modern look with all the warmth of traditional styling.

Of special interest is the wood-paneled family room that features a stone-face circular corner fireplace with a raised hearth and a built-in log storage bin.

This inviting and distinctive design affords an opportunity for a life style of warmth, flexibility and comfort.

TOTAL LIVING AREA: 2,660 sq. ft.
   Basement   1,700 sq. ft.
   Garage   530 sq. ft.

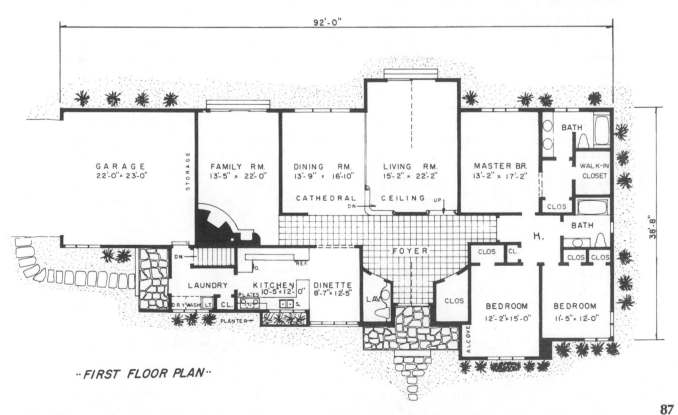

··FIRST FLOOR PLAN··

The Barcelona

Visitors to this home pass through wrought-iron gates into the entrance courtyard, along the walkway, flanked by plantings, to solid oak doors that open onto the impressive, spacious foyer. The exterior finish is white-washed stucco, a traditional material for Spanish colonial architecture.

The interior is enhanced by cathedral beamed ceilings in the living room, dining room and family rooms. The high ceilings make these very commodious rooms appear even larger. A free-standing, see-through fireplace is a special feature of the living and family rooms. Two full baths service the four spacious bedrooms, which have generous closet space and are secluded in one wing for privacy.

TOTAL LIVING AREA: Living area   3,150 sq. ft.
                   Laundry   126 sq. ft.
                   Garage   525 sq. ft.

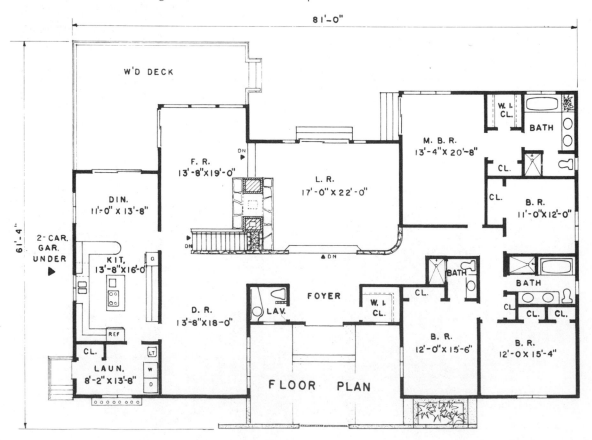

FLOOR PLAN

The Aventura

The interplay of varied rooflines, vertical red cedar siding, and glass panels create visual interest on the exterior of this handsome, contemporary three-bedroom ranch. Inside, the strategically placed kitchen is efficiently organized and conveniently located near the family room and next to the dining room.

Full glass paneled walls capture the view from the dinette and the dining room. The glass panels open to allow access to the outdoor living area.

The master bedroom suite features two walk-in closets and a private bath with a twin-basined vanity and a Roman tub. The other nearby bedrooms have ample wall space and are adjacent to the second bath.

TOTAL LIVING AREA: Living area   2,990 sq. ft.
                              Garage   570 sq. ft.

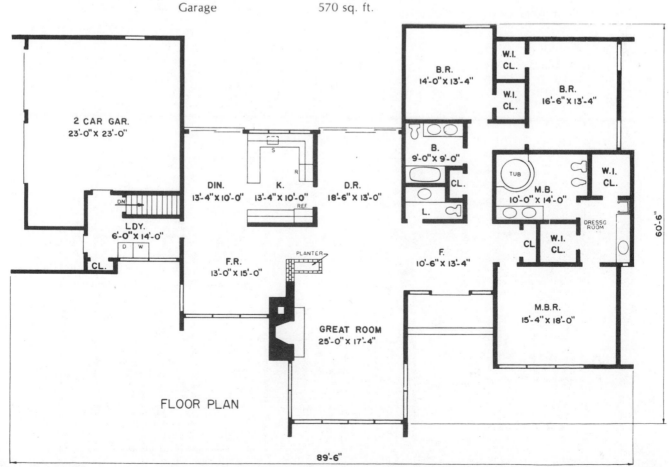

FLOOR PLAN

The Aspen

Modern and up-to-date is the best way to describe this spacious contemporary four bedroom ranch that is highlighted by the dramatic split-roof lines, fieldstone veneer, vertical redwood siding, clerestory and vertical window treatment. The double door entry gives a spacious feeling the moment you enter.

The living area includes a large sunken living room, dining room, kitchen-dinette, laundry and a wood paneled family room that features sliding-glass doors to the sun-deck and a see-through fireplace.

Designed to contribute to a feeling of personal luxury, the master bedroom suite has access to the outdoor wood deck, has two closets, one a walk-in, and a complete stall shower bath. The other three bedrooms are served by the main bath, which has a stall-shower, tub and a full length mirrored double-basin vanity.

AREA: First Floor   3193 sq. ft.
         Basement   1943 sq. ft.
         Garage   1250 sq. ft.

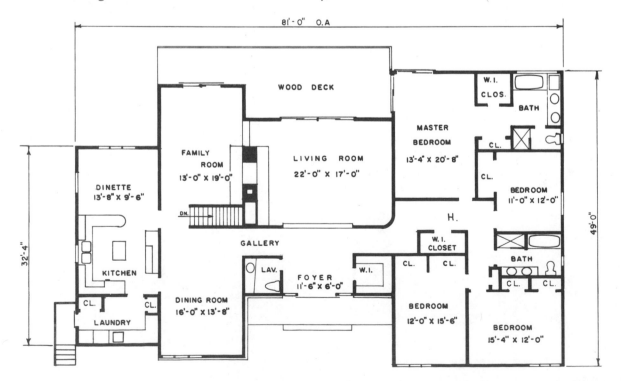

The Escondido

Spanish architecture has maintained a high level popularity through the years, and it is easy to see why. The use of varied materials, design elements and detailing always create a distinctive exterior. This one story "ranchero" is no exception. The stucco finish, arched casement windows, balconied windows and the double carved-paneled entrance doorway under the weather protected walkway are fully compatible with the requirements of contemporary American living.

The "cathedral-ceiling" living room spans 35 feet from the front to the rear patio, which is accessible by a pair of sliding glass doors. To the right is the kitchen-dinette that features an island counter, the laundry and an oversized two car garage with ample storage facilities.

The three bedroom sleeping area consists of a luxurious master suite with a room-size walk-in closet, three additional closets, sunken Roman bathtub, double basin vanity and tiled shower stall. The other two bedrooms are conveniently located to the compartmentalized main bath.

TOTAL LIVING AREA: 3,260 sq. ft.
Garage   680 sq. ft.

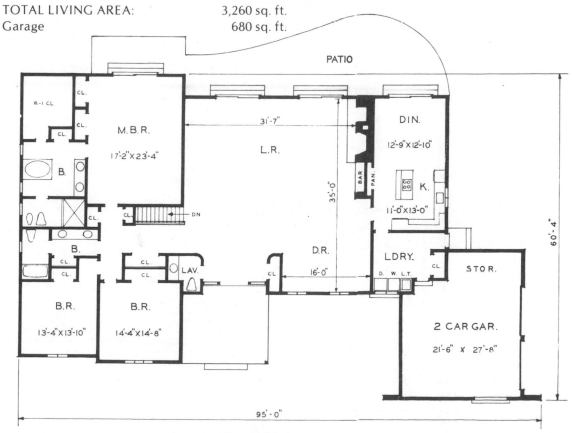

FIRST FLOOR PLAN

The Lancaster

There is a dash of modernism in the lines of this ranch home, but the contemporary style is essentially conservative, combining a variety of features and details popular in the past. There is a sunken living room and the combination open family room, dinette and kitchen. Three bedrooms, served by two complete baths, are effectively grouped around a central hall.

A ranch house is a strong favorite for older couples, growing families and do-it-yourselfers because the layout permits adaptations to individual life styles.

TOTAL LIVING AREA: Living area   2,488 sq. ft.
                    Laundry   180 sq. ft.
                    Garage   756 sq. ft.

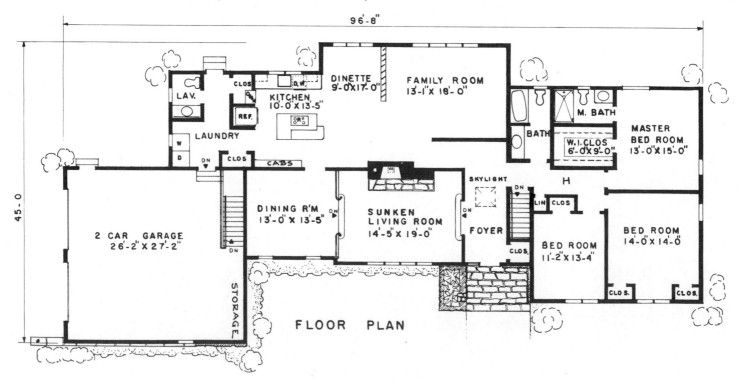

FLOOR PLAN

The Endicott

Sharp, clean lines of contemporary architecture are the distinctive feature of this four-bedroom ranch design. Vertical redwood siding, stone and glass produce a house front that is balanced and attractive. The double-door entry gives a look of elegance. The clean and simple style carries through to the inside. Cathedral ceilings rise above the sunken living room, with its open brick fireplace, and the family room and dining room. The sleeping wing is isolated for privacy; the master suite has two closets, double basin vanity, stall shower and sunken bathtub. Two complete bathrooms serve the other three bedrooms. Special features include a walk-in hall closet, first floor laundry room, U-shaped island kitchen and a wrap-around open sundeck.

TOTAL LIVING AREA: first floor   3,232 sq. ft.
                  Garage   978 sq. ft.

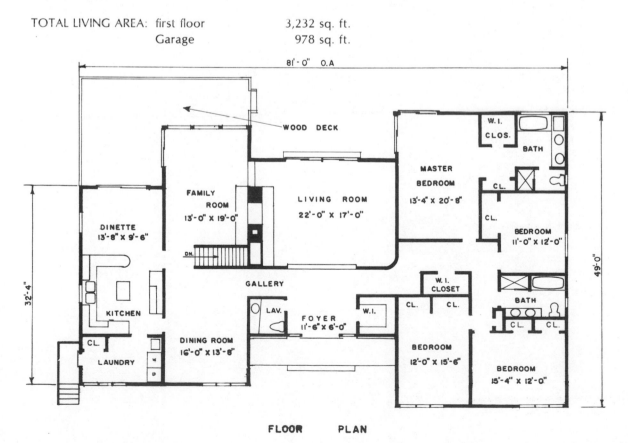

FLOOR PLAN

EXPANDABLE RANCH

The half-a-story usually refers to an attic which can be finished at the time of the original construction or later on. Often has master bedroom on first floor, children's bedrooms upstairs. Provides extra storage space under eaves. Has knee walls and sloping ceilings upstairs. Most one and one-half story houses have traditional details in the Cape Cod style.

The Innwood

This compact but ample-size, expansion-style house has won widespread popularity. The plan combines economy of space with efficiency of function. The step-saving kitchen makes every inch of space count, and the glass-enclosed dining porch affords a refreshing view of the yard. This home presents a neat exterior that will fit into any community; there is universal appeal in its freshness and charm.

The second floor, whether finished now or in the future, provides two bedrooms and bath.

TOTAL LIVING AREA: 925 sq. ft.

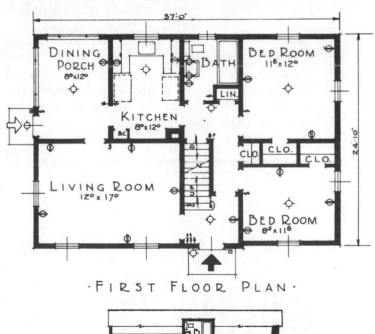

· FIRST FLOOR PLAN ·

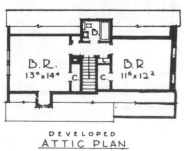

DEVELOPED
ATTIC PLAN

The Tennyson

Truly a dream cottage, with its fireplace walls pierced by diamond-paned windows turned to the street, this expansion house is as practical as a house can be. There's fireplace charm in the living room as well as outside, but this spacious room, with the squared dining room opening into it, offers plenty of space for easy hospitality. The kitchen's a step-saver, compact and efficient. Sharing a convenient bath are the two bedrooms, with three windows in one, and cross ventilation for both. Upstairs two more bedrooms are planned, each with lovely dormer alcoves. The second bathroom is over the kitchen plumbing for economy, and there's another linen closet upstairs to save every extra step.

AREA: First floor   990 sq. ft.
         Second floor   475 sq. ft.

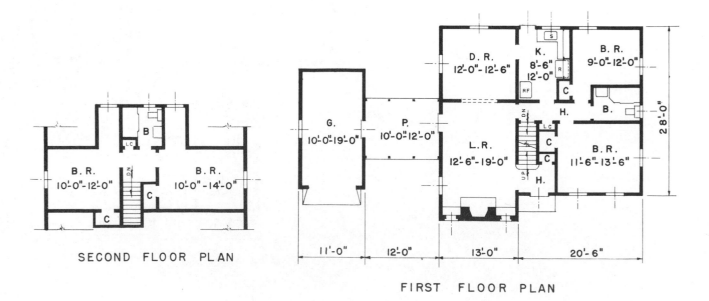

SECOND FLOOR PLAN

FIRST FLOOR PLAN

The Dennis

"Deceiving looking" from the exterior, within lie four large bedrooms with ample closets.

Two full baths are conveniently located outside the bedroom doors.

There is an abundant work area in the kitchen with its connecting dining area which seems to say roomy.

All rooms are sized for family living including the spacious living room.

The needs of comfort, convenience and practical living are combined in this home designed for a narrow lot.

AREA: First floor   832 sq. ft.
        Second floor   448 sq. ft.

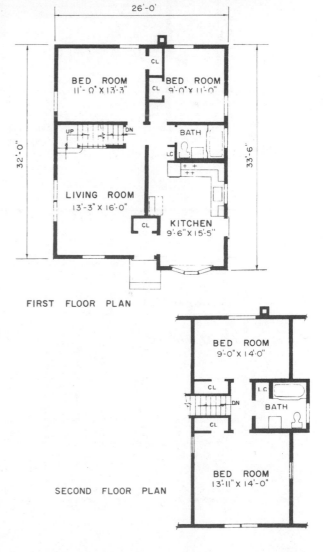

FIRST FLOOR PLAN

SECOND FLOOR PLAN

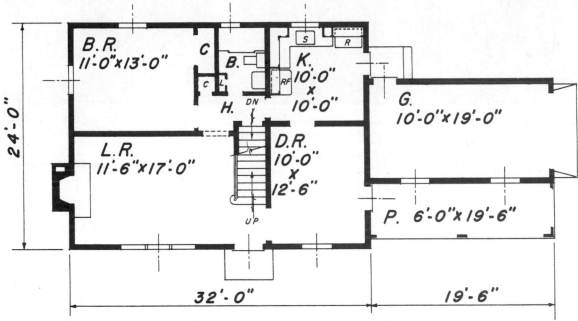

FIRST FLOOR PLAN

B.R.
11'-0"x13'-0"

C

B.

K.
10'-0"
x
10'-0"

S

R

RF

C L

H.

DN

G.
10'-0"x19'-0"

L.R.
11'-6"x17'-0"

D.R.
10'-0"
x
12'-6"

UP

P. 6'-0"x19'-6"

24'-0"

32'-0"

19'-6"

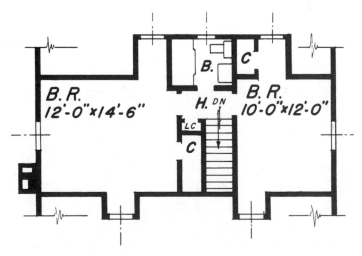

SECOND FLOOR PLAN

B.R.
12'-0"x14'-6"

B.

C

H. DN

B.R.
10'-0"x12'-0"

LC

C

The Preston

Comfort and privacy were given priority in designing this efficient and practical home. Housekeeping is easy because this home has a complete bedroom floor and a convenient, third bedroom downstairs, as well as two full baths.

There is a dining room with two exposures, one with a French door that opens onto a covered porch. The kitchen is accessible from the garage. The downstairs bathroom also is placed for convenience. Hall space has been held to a minimum for a square foot bonus in the downstairs rooms. Each of the two bedrooms on the upper floor has three exposures.

TOTAL LIVING AREA: First floor   768 sq. ft.
                including garage
                Second floor   500 sq. ft.

The Chatham

The compact arrangement of this five-room house with expansion attic means it can be built, without the breezeway and garage, on a lot that measures fewer than fifty feet.

A study of the plan reveals many features usually found only in larger homes. All of these special qualities have been incorporated in a surprisingly small area, a factor that means real economy. This is a small home, but one with considerable living space, suitable for either large or small families.

TOTAL LIVING AREA: First floor   1,105 sq. ft.
Second floor   470 sq. ft.

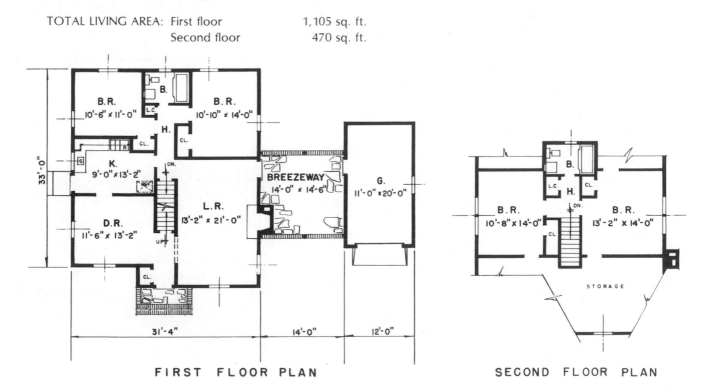

FIRST FLOOR PLAN   SECOND FLOOR PLAN

The Williamsburg

Traditional beauty and comfort in the Cape Cod style are set forth in this homey five room house with its expansion attic. A wonderful breezeway and garage expand this compact arrangement to provide the luxury look so typical of the New England Architecture.

AREA: First floor 870 sq. ft.
Second floor 473 sq. ft.

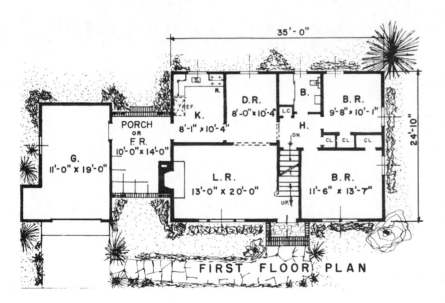

FIRST FLOOR PLAN

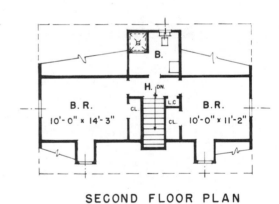

SECOND FLOOR PLAN

The Concord

This plan is something quite unusual—arranged to give many features not ordinarily obtained in a house with so conventional an appearance. Although we see a typical Cape Cod exterior, the service entrance and kitchen are in the front. In the rear, with large window areas overlooking a very up-to-date terrace, are the living room and dining room which take advantage of a view to the garden area. The two bedrooms and bath on the first floor provide ample space for the small family, and the second floor provides extensive area for expansion into two or more very large bedrooms and another full bath. A breezeway and attached garage complete this plan, which has every convenience for every day living.

AREA: First floor   1,054 sq. ft.
        Second floor   434 sq. ft.

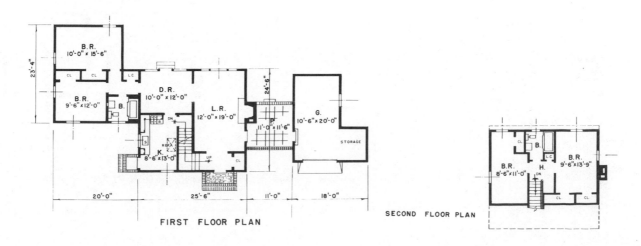

FIRST FLOOR PLAN

SECOND FLOOR PLAN

The Fieldstone

Quaint and picturesque in design, this home will be outstanding in any neighborhood. Compact and easy to care for, giving you the most for budget. A vestibule and coat closet offer hospitable welcome as you come in from the covered porch. The living room has two exposures and a door out to the breezeway. The fireplace keynotes a room of distinction.

On the other side, with windows on two sides, too, is the dining room, with an alcove for a built-in china cabinet. The kitchen is sunny, efficient and convenient to the cellar stairs.

At the rear are two bedrooms, featuring cross ventilation and super closets, and the bath between is family-sized. Two more dormered bedrooms can be added in the expansion attic, with the second bathroom utilizing the same plumbing stack of the one below for economy.

AREA: First floor   1,033 sq. ft.
       Second floor   550 sq. ft.

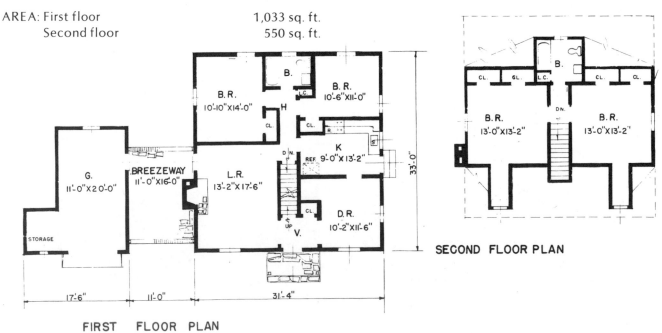

FIRST FLOOR PLAN

SECOND FLOOR PLAN

The Belmont

This well-planned ranch home presents an attractive face to those approaching it. Inside there is a comfortable living room and a dining room convenient to the step-saving kitchen. Three bedrooms are grouped to one side, and each has ample closet space. Plans have been made for a future upstairs bedroom and bath.

TOTAL LIVING AREA: First floor   1,430 sq. ft.
                       Second floor   439 sq. ft.

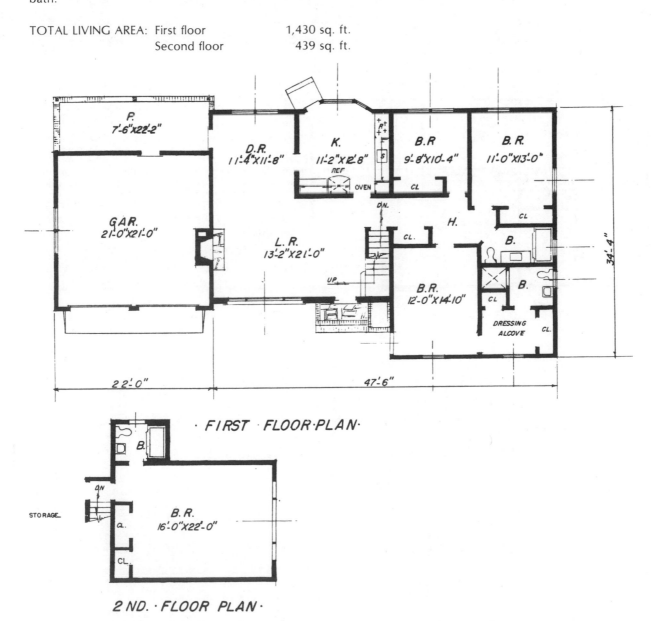

· FIRST ·FLOOR·PLAN·

· 2 ND. ·FLOOR PLAN·

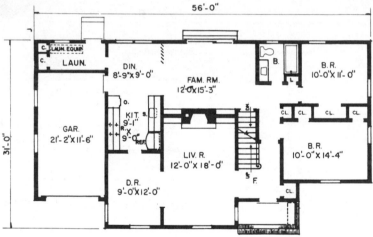

FIRST FLOOR PLAN

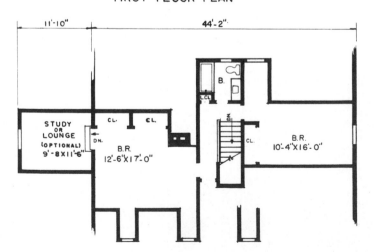

SECOND FLOOR PLAN

The Collier

This charming New England Cape Cod home is ideal for the growing family. There is a full size living room with fireplace and book shelves, dining room, and a large eating space in the kitchen-dinette. This lovely home also has a family room that opens directly to a patio, the rear yard, and garden area. Directly off the main foyer are two bedrooms with plenty of closet space, and a bath. A good-sized laundry room with access to the yard is located off the dinette area.

The first floor bath, immediately adjacent to the bedrooms and family room, is convenient enough to be used as a guest powder room. There is extensive closet space for guests.

When the family expands, the second floor can be finished into two king-size rooms and a private bath for the children.

TOTAL LIVING AREA: First floor   1,285 sq. ft.
Second floor   665 sq. ft.

The Sherwood

The brick planting bed is shadowed by a projecting gable face which forms wonderful weather protection for the entrance platform. This, combined with high, bright corner windows and a horizontal wood rail fence which separates the breezeway and garage, forms a pleasing exterior. The equally pleasant arrangement of interior plan combines comfort and convenience for perfect living. A full complement of rooms on the first floor, including two bedrooms and bath, are supplemented by an additional two rooms and bath on the second floor. So much living space in so small an appearing exterior is truly amazing. The living room with its specially arranged fireplace location and large corner of window area presents an immediate touch of "something different", which everyone is looking for these days.

AREA: First floor   1104 sq. ft.
       Second floor   570 sq. ft.
       Basement   1110 sq. ft.
       Garage   286 sq. ft.

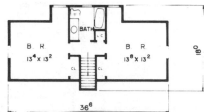

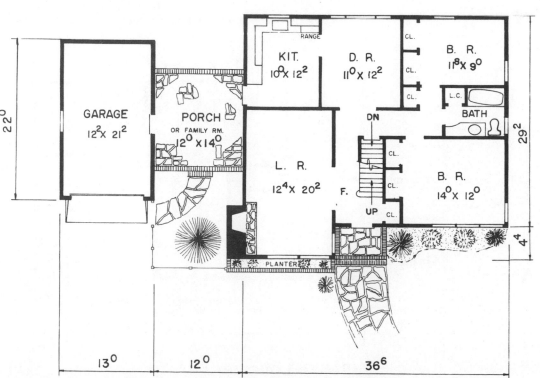

The Cornell

A pleasant combination of the old and the new is expressed in this home's warmth of feeling on the exterior and its convenience of planning on the interior. A separate entrance hall including guest closet and stair to the second floor starts out the plan. As this hall extends back it provides convenient passage to living room, kitchen, basement, bedrooms, and bath respectively. The living room features a full size real fireplace, lots of floor space and entrance to a neat breezeway. The breezeway, in addition to being a wonderful place for relaxing on summer evenings, performs the satisfying function of protecting passage to and from the attached garage in stormy weather.

AREA First floor   1186 sq. ft.
   Second floor   600 sq. ft.

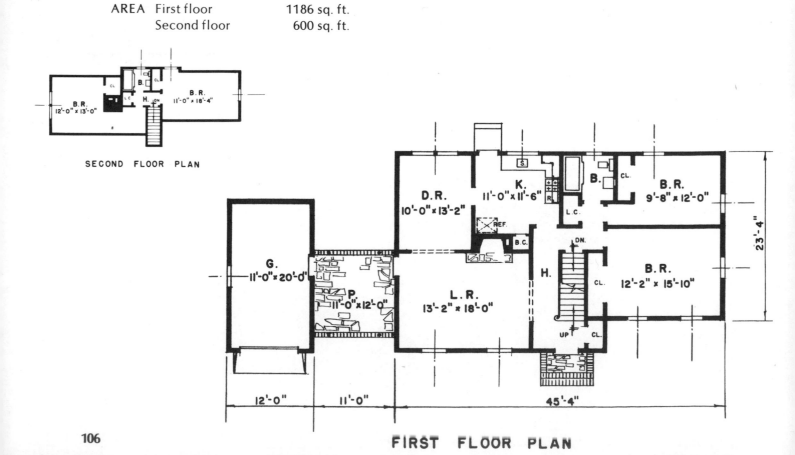

SECOND FLOOR PLAN

FIRST FLOOR PLAN

The Princeton

Here's a simple design that offers complete living on one floor, with an opportunity of utilizing the expansion space upstairs for additional living area, if so desired. The entrance foyer features a dramatic cathedral ceiling. This is a comfortable two bedroom house for a retired couple who no longer require a large home or one of economy and efficiency for a younger couple with one or two children, since it can be expanded from two to four bedrooms as needed.

AREA: First floor   1,300 sq. ft.
        Second floor   600 sq. ft.

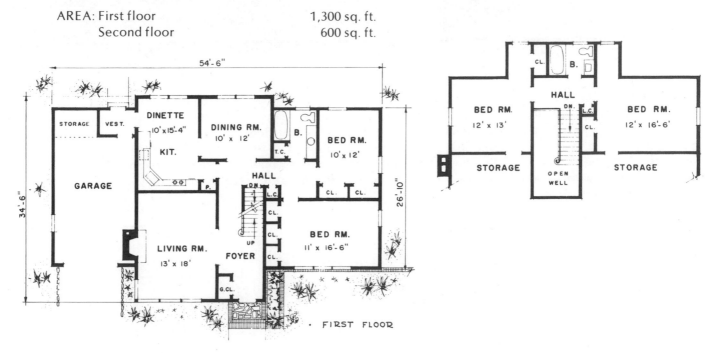

FIRST FLOOR

The Ashton

This expansion ranch home will be a welcome addition to any neighborhood. Inside, the living room connects through an arch to the dining room and is ideal for both formal and informal entertaining. The kitchen offers good working space for meal preparation. A large bedroom, study and full bathroom complete the spacious first floor. Upstairs, there is provision for two more, unusually roomy bedrooms, and a second bathroom.

TOTAL LIVING AREA: First floor   1,371 sq. ft.
   Second floor   800 sq. ft.

STUDY
12'-0" x 12'-6"

K.
11'-4" x 12'-0"

D. R.
11'-4" x 12'-6"

P
10'-0" x 15'-0"

B.

H.

L. R.
13'-4" x 23'-0"

G.
19'-0" x 21'-0"

B. R.
15'-0" x 17'-6"

F.

42'-10"

21'-6"

38'-0"

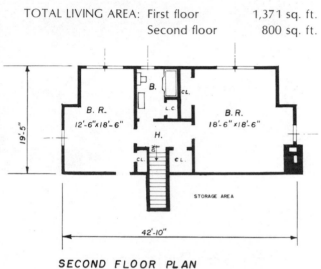

B. R.
12'-6" x 18'-6"

B. R.
18'-6" x 18'-6"

B.

H.

STORAGE AREA

19'-5"

42'-10"

SECOND FLOOR PLAN

"A cozy little home all our own" is the dream of most families. This is as cozy a home as you'll find, yet it is not condensed down to doll-house size. Waste space has been kept to an absolute minimum without sacrificing convenience and comfort. This plan includes such features as an entrance vestibule, a center-core hall for good circulation, loads of closets, large kitchen with separate dining area and access directly to the garage, basement and porch, not to mention the large living room with an open stair to a future expansion attic. This attic area has space for two more large bedrooms and a full bath.

The Drake

AREA: First floor   1,170 sq. ft.
   Second floor   756 sq. ft.

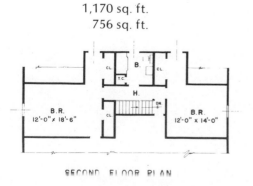

B. R.
12'-0" x 18'-6"

B.

B. R.
12'-0" x 14'-0"

H.

SECOND FLOOR PLAN

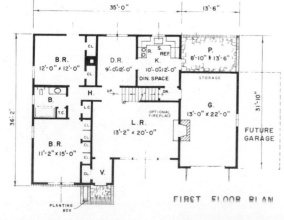

B. R.
12'-0" x 12'-0"

D. R.
9'-0" x 12'-0"

K.
10'-0" x 12'-0"

P.
8'-10" x 13'-6"

DIN. SPACE

STORAGE

H.

B.

L. R.
13'-2" x 20'-0"

G.
13'-0" x 22'-0"

FUTURE GARAGE

OPTIONAL FIREPLACE

B. R.
11'-2" x 15'-0"

V.

PLANTING BOX

35'-0"

13'-6"

36'-2"

31'-10"

FIRST FLOOR PLAN

The Ponderosa

Once past the courtyard of this home, the visitor enters a palatial, two-story, circular foyer with stairs that lead to the two bedrooms on the second floor. Ahead is the living room, with a fireplace that is also open to the equal-sized family room, which features a beamed ceiling. The efficient kitchen has a cooking island and extensive cabinets and working space. Three bedrooms, served by two full bathrooms, are secluded on the opposite side of the house.

TOTAL LIVING AREA:
First floor	3,090 sq. ft.	
Second floor	676 sq. ft.	
Garage	552 sq. ft.	

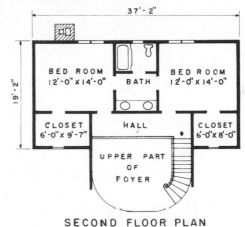

SECOND FLOOR PLAN

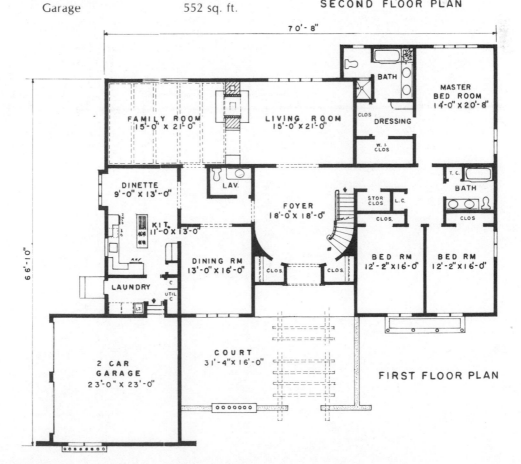

FIRST FLOOR PLAN

The Allen

All the charm of the traditional Cape Cod house has been recaptured in this story and a half house of fieldstone and siding. Though the house, as it appears in the rendering, is almost 80' long, and perfect for a corner lot, it could be built on a 60' frontage by eliminating the garage and porch, bringing it down to an overall length of 46'. Downstairs, there are two large bedrooms. A bath, well located off the front hall, serves also as a guest lavatory. A spacious, well lighted kitchen makes homecoming a joy. The dining room opens to the porch for cheerful summer suppers. A wide arch joins living and dining areas, and a handsome fireplace suggests unusual and cozy furniture groupings. On the dormered second floor there are two tremendous bedrooms and another full bath, to be finished as you need them, and all bedrooms enjoy two exposures.

AREA: First floor   1,316 sq. ft.
        Second floor   636 sq. ft.

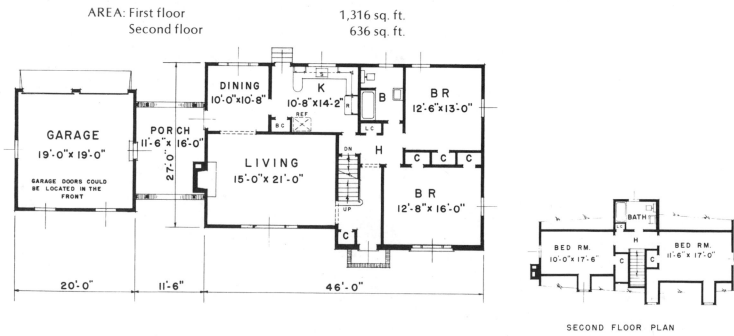

SECOND FLOOR PLAN

The Framingham

Quaint and picturesque in design, this home will be outstanding in any neighborhood . . . Compact and easy to care for, giving you the most for your budget . . . A foyer and coat closet offer hospitable welcome as you come in from the covered porch . . . The living room has two exposures and adjoins both the dining room and family room . . . the fireplace keynotes a room of distinction . . . The kitchen-family room is sunny, efficient and convenient to the rear yard . . . Two or three bedrooms, depending on personal requirements, featuring cross ventilation and super closets complete the first floor . . . Two more dormered bedrooms can be added in the expansion attic, with second bathroom utilizing the same plumbing stack of the one below for economy.

AREA: First floor   1,420 sq. ft.
        Second floor   560 sq. ft.

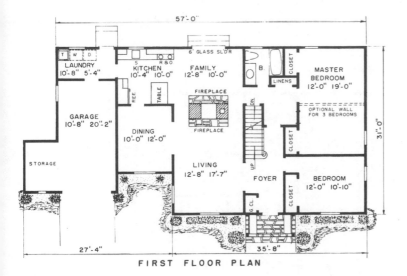

FIRST FLOOR PLAN

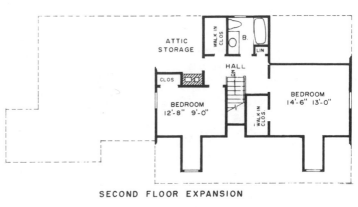

SECOND FLOOR EXPANSION

The Cameron

The luxurious entrance hall featured in this home is the introduction to an over-all plan for wonderful living in modern day style. The recessed entry is flanked by closets on either side, and the open stair lends an immediate impression of beauty and spaciousness. Extending beyond the entry hall is another small hall area which provides direct access to bedrooms, bath and kitchen. Closet space is abundant on both floors. The two rooms on the second floor of this plan are the nicest we have ever seen in a one and one-half story home. There is practically full ceiling height for the entire room area, and there are none of the unsightly breaks which usually occur in these "attic" rooms.

AREA: First floor   1,446 sq. ft.
            Second floor   619 sq. ft.

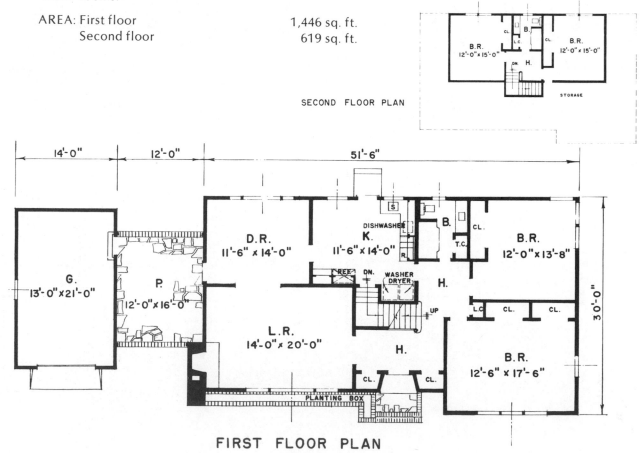

SECOND FLOOR PLAN

FIRST FLOOR PLAN

The Nantucket

This long, low, rambling dwelling appears to be a conventional ranch, but has two extra bedrooms and a bath upstairs . . . living room has a large picture window set in a box bay . . . beyond the living room is the dining room, entered through an arched opening . . . family room, kitchen, laundry room are in line in the back part of the house . . . corner fireplace in the living room is visible from the foyer . . . a hall leads to three bedrooms and two baths on the first floor. The second floor can be added at a later date.

AREA: 1st floor   1772 sq. ft.
        2nd floor   483 sq. ft.

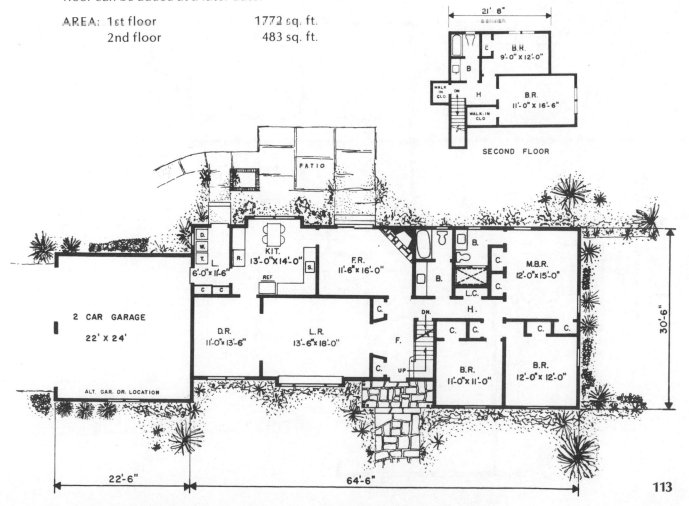

The Winslow

Here is the ideal home for the growing family.

This home with its overall dimension of 60' can be built on most 75' lots.

Note the desirable location of the family room, directly off the foyer and also adjacent to the dinette. This room, complete with large sliding doors and early American fireplace, will be one of the most used rooms in the house.

Connecting the kitchen and two car garage is a combination laundry-mud room, ideal for mother and children alike.

The living room with its large cottage windows affords maximum wall space for furniture arrangement.

The second floor affords two king size bedrooms, including two oversized closets in each room, and bath. This area can be finished during construction or as the family grows.

AREA: First floor   1,810 sq. ft.
          Second floor   650 sq. ft.

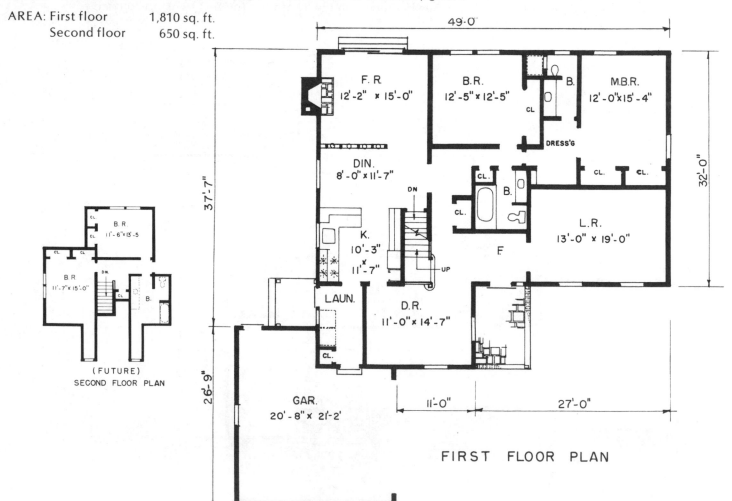

(FUTURE)
SECOND FLOOR PLAN

FIRST FLOOR PLAN

The Vancouver

Reminiscent of French chateau architecture, this one and one-half story, traditional home has the quiet dignity of country living. Entrance to this lovely home is through a garden court, and the double door entry leads straight ahead to the spacious living-room. The kitchen-dinette is designed for every modern built-in convenience, and its size makes meal preparation much easier; adjacent to it is the wood-paneled family room that features a raised-hearth fireplace and sliding glass doors to the rear patio. The three bedrooms are of modest size, but the master has its own private stall shower bath, and one of the front bedrooms is fortunate to have a view of the front courtyard. Two additional bedrooms and bath can be built on the second floor, at a future date, if so desired.

TOTAL LIVING AREA: 2,300 sq. ft.
Second floor 493 sq. ft.
Garage 500 sq. ft.

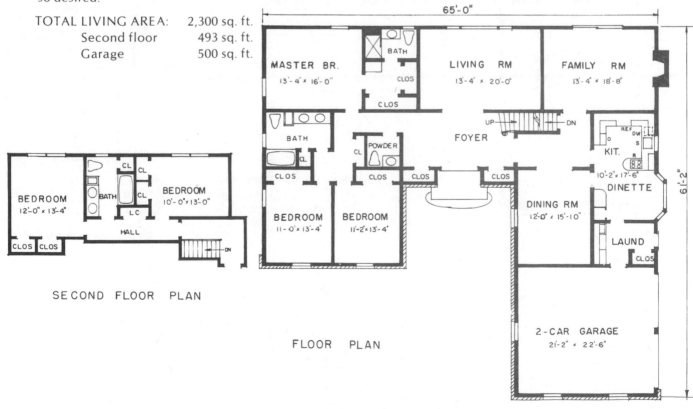

SECOND FLOOR PLAN

FLOOR PLAN

The Yarborough

The covered front portico exemplifies Colonial grace, together with brick veneer, wood shingles, board and batten vertical siding and shuttered windows to give this one and one-half story house a feeling of timeless beauty. The three car garage features a stair to the basement. Entering the front door is a spacious foyer with twin coat closets. Visible from the foyer is a formal sunken living room with circular bay window and a built-in window seat. The gallery offers a full view of the living room below by means of a knee high wrought iron railing. The traditional fireplace is located in the family room and is "backed-up" by another fireplace that graces the luxury of the master suite.

The attractive open stairway, with wrought iron railing and landing at the half point, leads to the additional three bedrooms on the second floor which may be finished at a later date, if so desired.

AREA: First floor   2,800 sq. ft.
          Second floor   1,130 sq. ft.
          Garage   750 sq. ft.

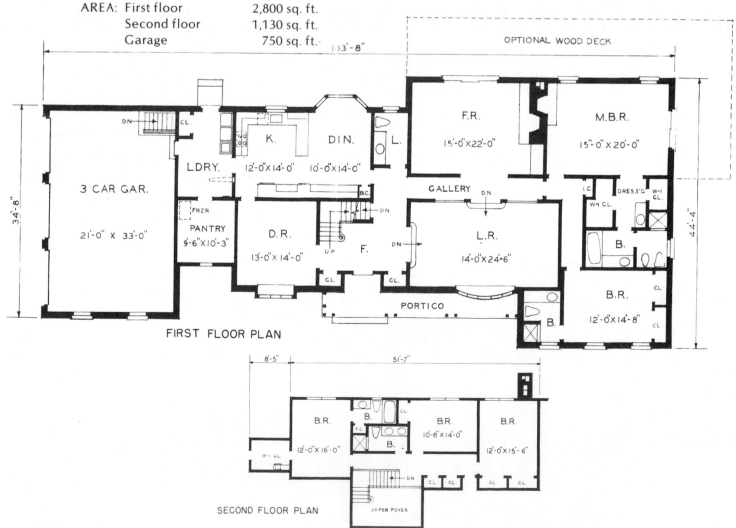

FIRST FLOOR PLAN

SECOND FLOOR PLAN

The Wilshire

A flavor of French Provincial architecture is emphasized in this one and one-half story design by the steep roof lines, the massive chimney and the distinctive double entrance doors.

To the right of the spacious foyer is the sunken living room, and to the rear is the wood-paneled family room, which features a corner brick fireplace and a triple sliding glass door that leads to the rear terrace. The U-shaped kitchen and dinette with sliding doors to the rear are a homemaker's delight. A spare room off the laundry and two car garage may be used as a maid's quarters or hobby room.

Two bedrooms, each with its own private bath, complete the first floor.

Upstairs, the two bedrooms and bath which can be finished at a later date, if so desired, are reached by an attractive open-well staircase

AREA: First floor   2,290 sq. ft.
       Second floor   630 sq. ft.
       Garage   420 sq. ft.

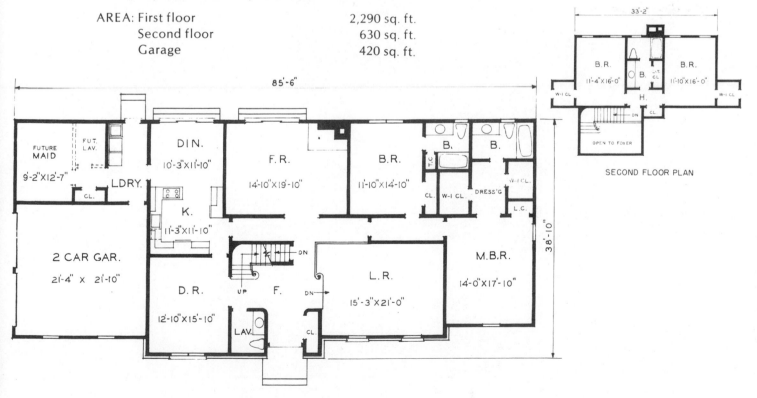

FIRST FLOOR PLAN

VACATION AND LEISURE-TIME HOMES

Whatever your taste, whatever your budget, the following designs for vacation or leisure-time living offer a change from everyday patterns. Today—more than ever before, Americans are investing in the future in a "second" home—it pays dividends in pleasure and relaxation, while increasing in value over the years.

Whatever your choice, the following designs will intrigue your imagination and complement your budget.

The Brookes

Are you looking for a house suitable to a hillside or mountain lake? Look no further, for here is the ideal house, incorporating substantial size and solidity with the informality of a vacation hideaway.

Two bedrooms, cheery efficient kitchen with easy access to dining area and outdoor patio combined with front to back living room complete with oversized fireplace and balcony suggest the varied use of this house. Downstairs is the perfect open room for children's play or family parties accessible to the lower outside area for picnics and family gatherings.

TOTAL LIVING AREA: 855 sq. ft.

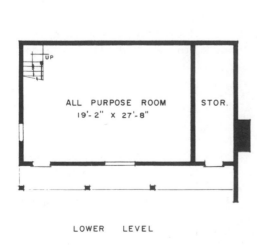

LOWER LEVEL

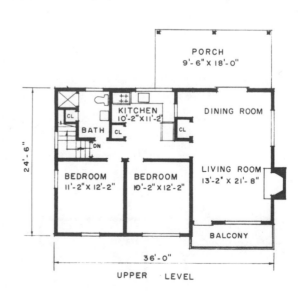

UPPER LEVEL

The Quebec

Kept to a minimum for the sake of a limited budget, this compact contemporary two bedroom design is a simple rectangle, 24' x 36', featuring a gentle sloping saddle roof taking in a carport on one side and a porch on the other.

The indoor-outdoor character of the plan is increased by the glass wall and door between the living-dining area and the porch.

For year-round living, provision is made for heating and/or cooling unit in the utility room by means of ductwork or, if desired, by electric heating coils in the ceiling, baseboard radiation or wall units.

For the growing number of families who desire to own a retirement or "minimum" home, there isn't much doubt about the suitability of this design.

AREA:	First floor	864 sq. ft.
	Porch	240 sq. ft.
	Carport & Storage	350 sq. ft.

The Hilltop

The A-frame design, synonymous with vacation living, has received many architectural treatments. Here is another variation which proves that there is something new under the sun — 25' x 25' square floor plan with a prow-shaped two-story glass expanse facing a wrap-around wood sun deck to take full advantage of your favorite view. The living area is quite dramatic with an exposed wood beam cathedral ceiling, a large rugged stone-wall corner fireplace, raised brick hearth with a dome-shaped hood, plank flooring, and sliding glass doors accessible to the deck.

Whatever your motive, whether it be a retreat in the woods, a cottage on the lake or a beach house by the shore, this design is all "decked out" for convenient living and complete relaxation.

AREA:	First floor	625 sq. ft.
	Second floor	450 sq. ft.
	Deck	675 sq. ft.

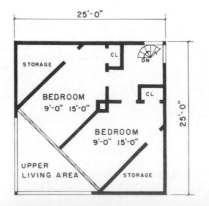

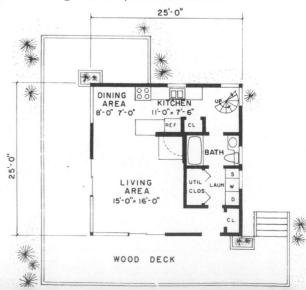

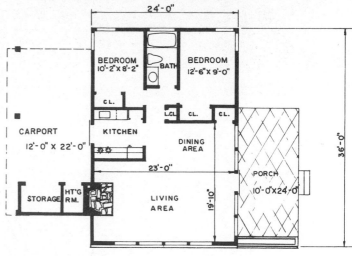

FIRST FLOOR PLAN

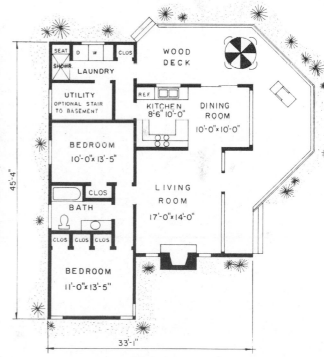

The Harvey Cedars

This contemporary two bedroom ranch design is ideal for retirement — not so large that it would burden a housekeeper, but with plenty of room when the grandchildren come to visit, and excellent for a second home — a lakeside or mountain retreat for all seasons.

The living room is accented by the massive fieldstone fireplace flanked on both sides from floor to ceiling with vertical windows and glass panels, cathedral ceiling and a full wall of windows to take advantage of a good near or distant view.

If convenient, economical and comfortable living is of primary importance, this contemporary ranch-style design that takes advantage of surrounding scenery in almost any direction may be just the new home for you.

AREA: First floor   1,105 sq. ft.
       Deck   476 sq. ft.

The Birchwood

Simple lines and vertical red cedar siding make this design suitable for any site. The plan features provision for solar-heated hot water produced by collector plates that can be installed on either the front or rear slope of the main roof, depending on the house orientation.

The main floor contains the large living room, a bedroom with cross-ventilation, and the kitchen. A lavatory is accessible from the kitchen and the bedroom. The screened-in porch, or breezeway, provides access between the house and the garage, which may be used as a boat house.

A circular staircase connects the living room with the overlooking balcony, which provides access to the sundeck and to the two bedrooms connected by a complete stall-shower bath.

TOTAL LIVING AREA:
First floor	746 sq. ft.
Second floor	392 sq. ft.
Garage	235 sq. ft.
Porch	168 sq. ft.

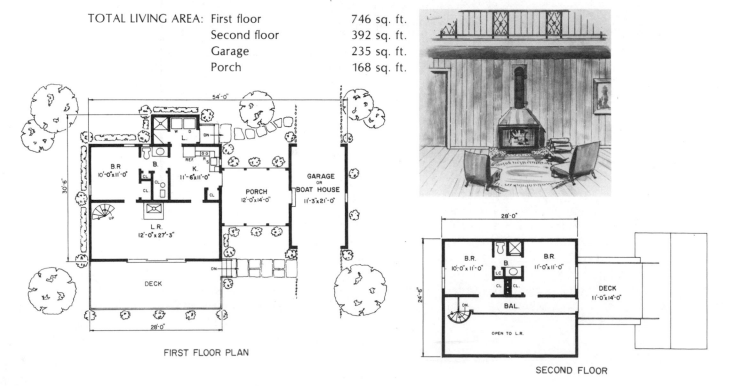

FIRST FLOOR PLAN

SECOND FLOOR

The Baywood

The open plan of this A-frame has a rustic cathedral ceiling sheathed throughout in attractive V-joint redwood decking and wood paneled walls. The living-dining area, 24 feet long, has a log-burning stone fireplace. The generous use of glass sliding doors merges the interior with the sun deck for easy outdoor living and entertaining.

The second floor "loft" bedroom features two closets and may be a guest or hobby room. A stair balcony overlooks the living area and leads to a stall-shower bath.

This distinctive design is tailored to family needs and can easily accommodate weekend guests.

TOTAL LIVING AREA: First floor   938 sq. ft.
                 Loft (second) floor   245 sq. ft.

LOFT PLAN

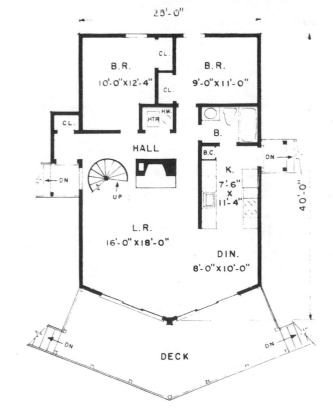

· FIRST FLOOR ·

The Alden

A great deal of living is designed into this compact ranch plan.

Ideal for a lake or beach home, this may well fit on a suburban lot.

The clean sweeping contemporary lines of the exterior architecture foretell the free open living pattern to be established within.

A full basement is provided in this plan, and there is ample space for play room, utilities, workshop and many other facilities.

TOTAL LIVING AREA: 1,100 sq. ft.
(excl. breezeway and garage).

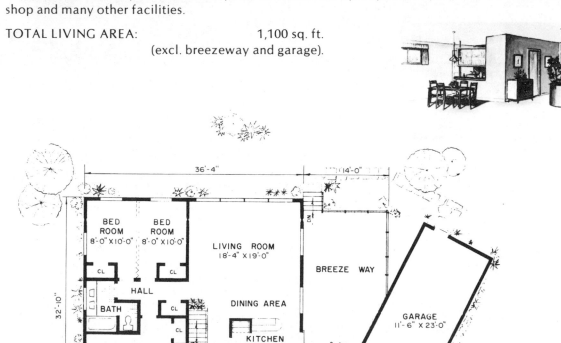

FLOOR PLAN

The Chelsea

This condensed version of a modern ranch home still includes a full complement of rooms. Three bedrooms, separate dining area; and a vestibule entrance with a guest closet are offered in this plan. The generous amount of closet space is unusual in so small a home. Every square inch of floor area is put to use; the working drawings will show a basementless alternate layout that includes a carport and a storage section.

TOTAL LIVING AREA: 960 sq. ft.

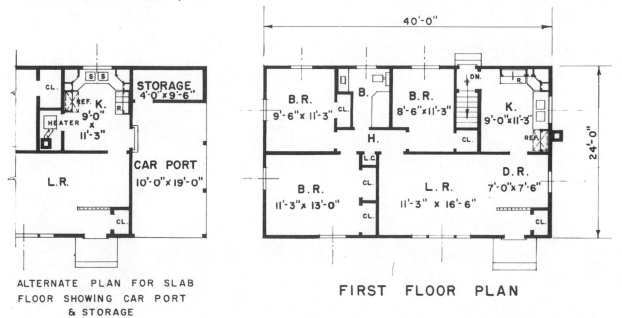

ALTERNATE PLAN FOR SLAB
FLOOR SHOWING CAR PORT
& STORAGE

FIRST FLOOR PLAN

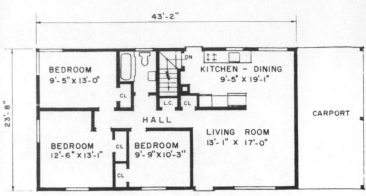

FIRST FLOOR

The Rowland

Ranch style economy is the keynote of this condensed version of today's popular home. A full complement of rooms including 3 bedrooms, spacious kitchen dining area and wonderful closet space are important features of this house. Also notice the direct access from the kitchen to outside and to the full cellar. Available with carport, this compact ranch is fully employed to the best use.

TOTAL LIVING AREA: 1,031 sq. ft.

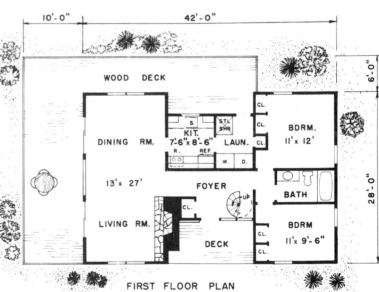

FIRST FLOOR PLAN

The Delaware

Today, more than ever before, American families are investing in the future, and one of the most attractive investments is a second home. This "away-from-home" modified chalet-style design offers an abundance of appealing features for indoor or outdoor easy and relaxed living.

The isolated location of the second floor "loft" suggests its use as a guest room or a place for painting or hobby; it features two closets, a balcony that overlooks the living room below, and a private outdoor balcony for sunning, sleeping or viewing.

With only 1,028 square feet of livable space on the first floor this house is designed for economy in construction and is well suited for carefree year round living.

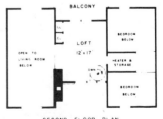

SECOND FLOOR PLAN

AREA:	First floor	1,028 sq. ft.
	Second floor	245 sq. ft.
	Deck	755 sq. ft.

126

The Seaview

The casual air and the easy care associated with vacation life are assured by the rough-cut vertical siding, stained wood roof shingles, interior wood-paneled walls and the rugged field-stone chimney by the contemporary exterior styling of this design.

Full advantage of the open-plan concept has been taken in the living area by the design treatment of the sunken conversation pit with built-in bench seating facing an open fireplace.

The isolated location of the second-floor loft suggests its use as a guest room, painting, sewing or hobby room. It features two closets and overlooks the living area below.

Although the plan is of basementless design, a full or partial basement is possible if the terrain or physical land characteristics permit, with the stairway from the laundry room.

This plan, with its natural wood exterior and interior, simple design and economical requirements, brings the second home within the reach of many families.

AREA: First floor   1,055 sq. ft.
         Second floor   250 sq. ft.
         Deck   755 sq. ft.

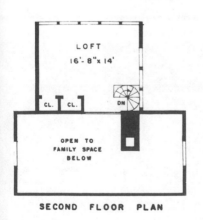

SECOND FLOOR PLAN

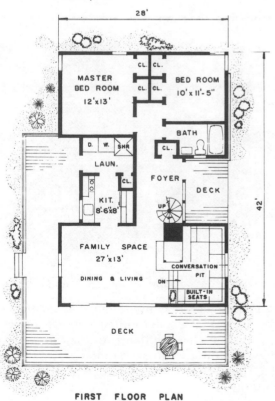

FIRST FLOOR PLAN

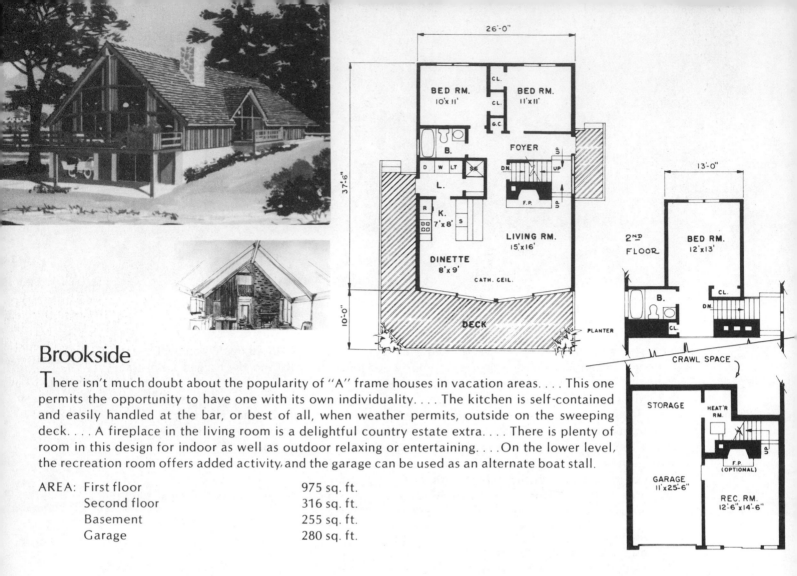

Brookside

There isn't much doubt about the popularity of "A" frame houses in vacation areas. . . . This one permits the opportunity to have one with its own individuality. . . . The kitchen is self-contained and easily handled at the bar, or best of all, when weather permits, outside on the sweeping deck. . . . A fireplace in the living room is a delightful country estate extra. . . . There is plenty of room in this design for indoor as well as outdoor relaxing or entertaining. . . . On the lower level, the recreation room offers added activity, and the garage can be used as an alternate boat stall.

AREA:
First floor	975 sq. ft.
Second floor	316 sq. ft.
Basement	255 sq. ft.
Garage	280 sq. ft.

The Alpine

Modern and up-to-date is the best way to describe this design of a "second home" or a home for all seasons, which is highlighted by the dramatic split roofline, the exterior vertical siding and the massive interior stone-faced fireplace and chimney that rise majestically from the living area past the balcony, clerestory windows and through the shed roof.

Strictly contemporary in feeling, this leisure home is so basically right and appealing that it seems destined for indefinite popularity.

AREA:
First floor	960 sq. ft.
Second floor	580 sq. ft.
Wood deck	460 sq. ft.

The Yukon

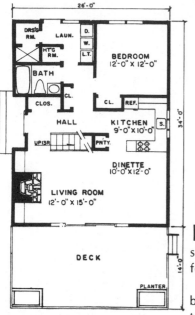

FIRST FLOOR PLAN

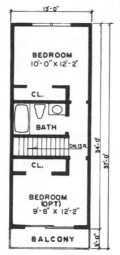

SECOND FLOOR PLAN

It is no wonder that the unique look of an A-Frame has proven to be a popular vacation design, since it is dramatic to look at, practical to live in and economical to build. The natural earthly feeling of this home would be ideal for a wooded or seaside lot in any neighborhood.

Highlights of this design are the fieldstone chimney that soars up through the roof, vertical boards and battens, stained red-cedar wood shingles and a red-wood sundeck that creates an interesting exterior.

For year-round living, provision is made for a supplemental heating unit in the utility room. Although the plan is of basementless design, a full basement is possible if the physical land characteristics permit, with the basement stair located under the main stair where the closet is now shown.

There is no doubt that this plan typifies the trend toward year-round use of vacation living and leisure activity.

AREA: First floor   881 sq. ft.
        Second floor   441 sq. ft.
        Deck   364 sq. ft.

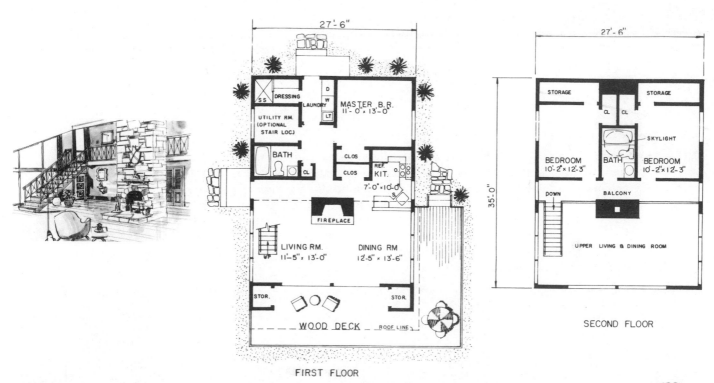

FIRST FLOOR

SECOND FLOOR

The Tahoe

Open planning is stressed by the interior of this design and it is kept rustic with exposed beams at the ceilings and wood paneled walls throughout.

The combination of living-dining area, 30' long, is most impressive with the generous use of glass, its cathedral ceiling, sliding-glass doors to the outdoor deck and cozy fireplace. Ample opportunity is offered by the wrap-around sun-deck to spend hours in the fresh air and make outdoor living, entertaining and serving a pleasurable event.

A dramatic wrought-iron spiral stairs leads upstairs to the balcony bedroom or "sleeping-loft" that may be used by a guest or as a place for painting or hobby.

Whatever your leisure activity, the specifics of this plan are "decked-out" for economy, convenient living and complete relaxation.

AREA: First floor   1,183 sq. ft.
   Second floor loft   210 sq. ft.
   Sun Deck   490 sq. ft.

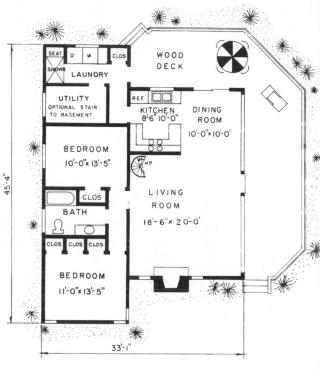

The Pocono

There is an unmistakable Provincial air to this unique leisure home.

The soaring "mansard" type roof is the dominant exterior feature of this design; it is enhanced by the massive fieldstone chimney, vertical V-joint red cedar siding, a sundeck that provides ample outdoor living space and stained wood roof shingles that comprise most of the sides of the building. For low maintenance costs, the interior throughout, except the bath, is of wood paneled walls.

To the growing number of families who today desire to own a "minimum" or second home, there isn't much doubt about the suitability of this design.

AREA: First floor   884 sq. ft.
   Second floor   442 sq. ft.
   Sundeck   364 sq. ft.

The Valley-View

The prow-Alpine roof of this A-frame design is enhanced by the triangular gable and upper deck over the carport. Open planning is stressed by the one large visual area which serves as the kitchen-dinette area and features a stone faced fireplace in the living room and the bedroom on the ground level.

The two bedrooms, each with its own deck, and bath on the second floor can be built at a later date, if so desired. For a high degree of livability and minimum maintenance requirements, there isn't much doubt about the suitability of this A-frame design.

AREA: First floor   868 sq. ft.
       Second floor   505 sq. ft.
       Covered & Open Patio   469 sq. ft.

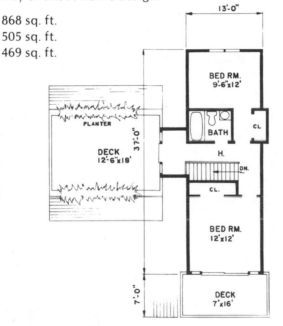

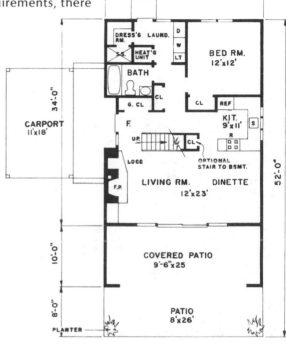

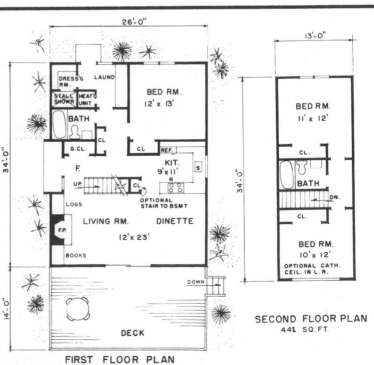

The Margate

This plan is at home with the great outdoors—it is designed to blend with the landscape and take full advantage of a beautiful view. The natural wood exterior of vertical boards of redwood, cedar or pine, the wood paneled interior, and the other economical construction requirements of this type of plan bring a second home within the reach of many families.

The exposed ceiling wood beams of the dinette-living area slope with the angle of the roof. This area runs the full width of the structure and takes full advantage of the unrestricted view through the all-glass facade and features an attractive log-burning fieldstone fireplace that takes the chill off cool nights. Two bedrooms with ample closets and wall space complete the layout.

There is only 1,040 square feet of livable area and 510 square feet of deck in this comfortable plan, and all of it is well planned and convenient to use.

TOTAL LIVING AREA: 1,040 sq. ft.
Deck   510 sq. ft.

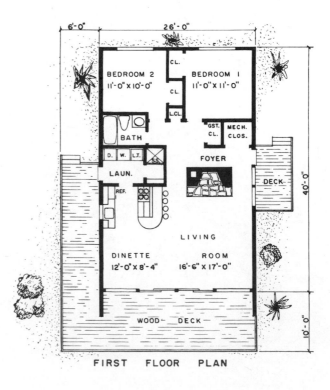

FIRST FLOOR PLAN

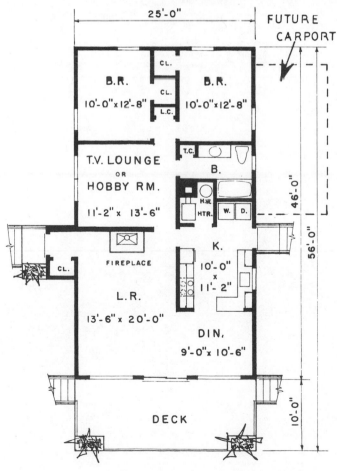

25'-0"

FUTURE CARPORT

B.R.
10'-0"x12'-8"

CL.
CL.
L.C.

B.R.
10'-0"x12'-8"

T.V. LOUNGE
OR
HOBBY RM.
11'-2" x 13'-6"

T.C.

B.

H.W.
HTR.

W. D.

FIREPLACE

CL.

L.R.
13'-6" x 20'-0"

K.
10'-0"
x
11'-2"

DIN.
9'-0"x 10'-6"

46'-0"

56'-0"

10'-0"

DECK

.. FLOOR PLAN

The Sagamore

This compact, two-bedroom design contains a habitable area of 1,175 square feet in a simple rectangle of 25 x 46 feet. The plan features a redwood sundeck, V joint vertical siding, and a gently sloping, asphalt-shingle saddle roof. Simple architectural lines and natural materials make this house suitable for any site.

Beyond the side entrance, the cathedral ceiling visually enlarges the living room area. The exposed ceiling beams extend beyond the almost all-glass front wall to support the roof overhang that partially shades the sundeck.

In addition to an ample modern kitchen, there are two moderate-sized bedrooms and a lounge area that is located for easy conversion to a third bedroom, if desired. This house could be a year-round home for most families.

A utility area, located near the kitchen, holds the water heater and heating/air conditioning unit. The plan is shown basementless, but a full basement is optional. The stairs would be built in place of the washer/dryer nook shown.

TOTAL LIVING AREA: First floor   1,175 sq. ft.
Sundeck   250 sq. ft.

The Sea-Girt

This simple contemporary vacation house of diagonal V-joint red wood siding is ideally suited for a wooded setting. It is a vacation house that contains all the basic elements of leisure living, without many of the frills and luxuries you might want in your year-round home.

The first floor contains a living and dining area with massive windows overlooking the scenery in all directions.

If a vacation house is in your plans, consider the long range economy and comfort of this design.

AREA: First floor   816 sq. ft.
        Second floor   528 sq. ft.
        Heater-Storage   72 sq. ft.
        Decks   342 sq. ft.

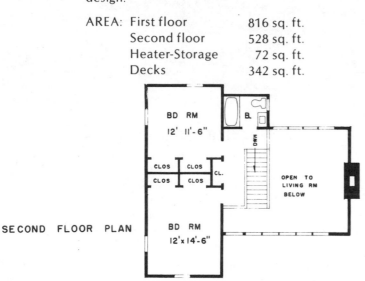

SECOND FLOOR PLAN

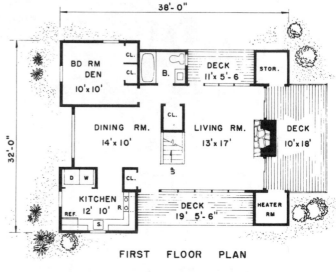

FIRST FLOOR PLAN

The Vacation Home

There is a great deal of eye appeal to the exterior of this very delightful A-frame design. The wrap-around, partially screened-in, sun drenched deck gives a choice of location for relaxing or entertaining from the large visual area of the second floor which serves as the living area. This is a basementless plan that has an electric heating unit for year-round living and has three bedrooms and two baths on the first floor.

AREA: First floor   676 sq. ft.
        Second floor   676 sq. ft.
        Sundeck: 356 sq. ft.
        Screened Porch   125 sq. ft.

The Camelot

Exciting exteriors, like this unique recreation house which suggests the Far East, sometimes can't be "themselves" in the suburbs, but come to life and are perfect for a picturesque building site in the woodlands or at the beach.

Whatever your motive, whether it be a retreat in the woods, a cottage on the lake, or a beach house by the shore, this design, all "decked out" with an oriental flavor, will answer your need for relaxation and that get-away-from-it-all leisure feeling

AREA: Living level   702 sq. ft.
         Bedroom level   702 sq. ft.

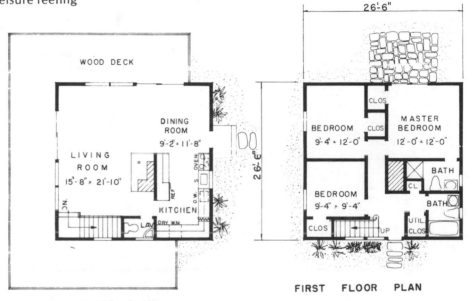

WOOD DECK

DINING ROOM
9'-2" x 11'-8"

LIVING ROOM
15'-8" x 21'-10"

KITCHEN

LAV.

SECOND FLOOR PLAN

26'-6"

CLOS

BEDROOM
9'-4" x 12'-0"

CLOS

MASTER BEDROOM
12'-0" x 12'-0"

BEDROOM
9'-4" x 9'-4"

CL

BATH

BATH

CLOS

UP

UTIL

CLOS

26'-6"

FIRST FLOOR PLAN

26'-0"

BED RM.
13'-0" x 9'-6"

MASTER BED RM.
12'-0" x 13'-6"

C

L.

BED RM.
9'-6" x 9'-6"

C.

HTG. CL.

B

CL.

UP

B

26'-0"

FIRST FLOOR PLAN

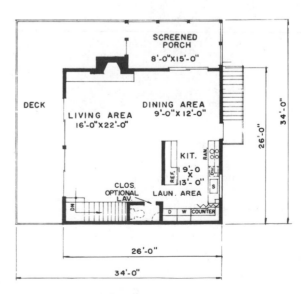

SCREENED PORCH
8'-0" x 15'-0"

DECK

DINING AREA
9'-0" x 12'-0"

LIVING AREA
16'-0" x 22'-0"

KIT.
9'-0" X 13'-0"

REF.

CLOS.
OPTIONAL LAV.

LAUN. AREA

DN

D W COUNTER

26'-0"

34'-0"

26'-0"

34'-0"

SECOND FLOOR PLAN

The Lake-Edge

I n this distinctive variation of the popular "A-frame," the structure is built in the conventional manner of wood studs, rafters and joists. The entire front facade is glass, making it a wonderful house for a view-endowed property, permitting sunshine to stream into the living area to create a cheerful outdoor atmosphere.

Although the plan is of basementless design, a full basement is possible with the basement stair located where the utility room is now located.

AREA: First level   962 sq. ft.
        Second level   578 sq. ft.
        Total   1,540 sq. ft.

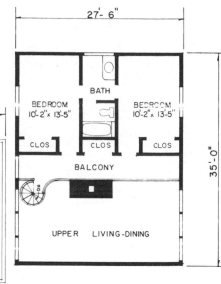

DRESS. — LND. — DRY — W — LT

UTILITY
OPTIONAL STAIR TO BASEMENT

MASTER BED.
11'-0" x 13'-0"

BATH — CL — CLOS — CLOS — REF — KIT

8'-0"

LIVING 11'-2" x 12'-4"

DINING 12'-5" x 12'-4"

DWARF WALL

10'-0"

W O O D   D E C K

27'-6"

BATH

BEDROOM 10'-2" x 13'-5"

BEDROOM 10'-2" x 13'-5"

CLOS   CLOS   CLOS

BALCONY

UPPER   LIVING-DINING

35'-0"

The Hide-away

W hether the setting reflects the majestic beauty of a winter scene or the tranquil splendor of a summer landscape, this A-frame design fills the bill for fun-time vacation or year round informal family living.

TOTAL LIVING AREA: First floor   884 sq. ft.
                    Second floor   441 sq. ft.

884 sq. ft.
441 sq. ft.

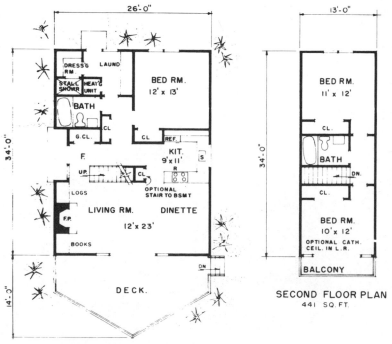

26'-0"

DRESS'G RM.   LAUND

STALL SHOWER   HEAT'G UNIT

BATH

BED RM. 12' x 13'

G.CL.   CL   CL   REF

F.

KIT. 9' x 11'

34'-0"

LOGS

UP

OPTIONAL STAIR TO BSMT

LIVING RM.   DINETTE
12' x 23'

F.P.

BOOKS

14'-0"

DN

D E C K.

FIRST FLOOR PLAN

13'-0"

BED RM. 11' x 12'

CL.

BATH

DN

CL.

BED RM. 10' x 12'
OPTIONAL CATH. CEIL. IN L.R.

BALCONY

34'-0"

SECOND FLOOR PLAN
441 SQ. FT.

136

The Beach Haven

The up-to-date modified contemporary exterior styling of this two-story design offers an eye-pleasing effect, which compliments the proportions of the dramatic interior layout.

Redwood boards and battens, striking roof lines, large unobstructed glass area in the front and rear of the living-dining area and the wrap-around wide sun deck give a choice of locations for sunning and relaxing.

The combination living and dining area is most impressive with the generous use of glass, its cathedral ceiling, double pair of sliding doors on the side, cozy fireplace and the charm and intrigue of the overhanging balcony. A dramatic set of wrought iron spiral stairs lead up to the second floor.

The second floor, which may be finished at a later date, consists of two bedrooms, with twin-beds or bunk-house sleeping arrangement, ample closet space, and a connecting bath with mechanical ventilation and ceiling skylight.

This distinctive design is geared for the comfortable seclusion of couples or small families to enjoy carefree year-round living with all the conveniences found in homes costing much more.

AREA: First floor   998 sq. ft.
        Second floor   548 sq. ft.
        Sun Deck   550 sq. ft.

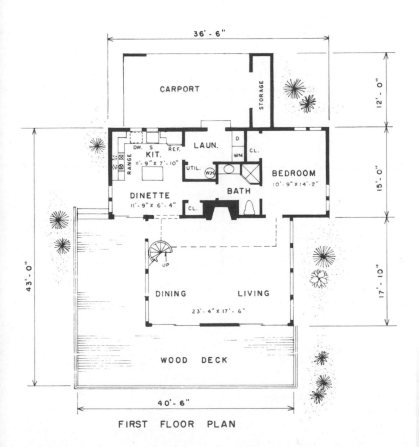

FIRST FLOOR PLAN

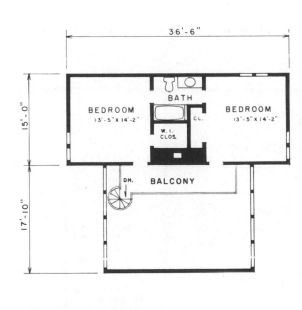

SECOND FLOOR PLAN

The Timber-wood

The front entry of this cedar-clad home is sheltered by a shed roof. Featured inside is a greenhouse, which, if planned to face south, captures the heat of the sun and functions as a solarium. This house is energy efficient; warm air rises from the lower level along the sloping ceiling to the second floor. If you are considering solar heating, orient this house so the saltbox roof can serve as the location for the solar collectors.

TOTAL LIVING AREA:

First floor	836 sq. ft.
Second floor	475 sq. ft.
Basement	836 sq. ft.
Laundry	130 sq. ft.
Garage	308 sq. ft.

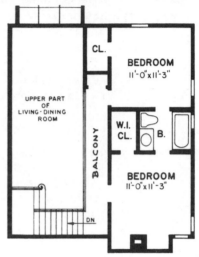

SECOND FLOOR

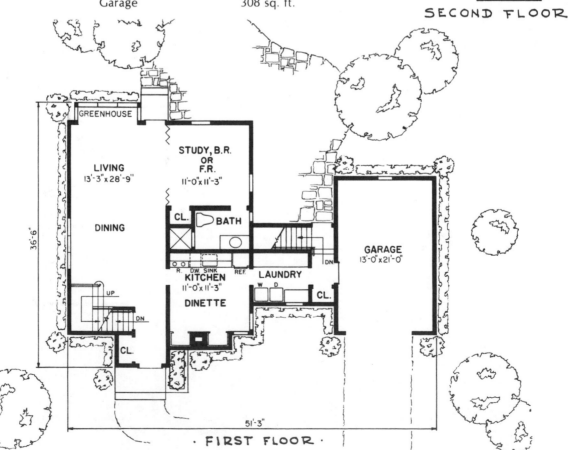

· FIRST FLOOR ·

The Barnegat

Economy, beauty and simplicity meet in this contemporary year-round or vacation home. Although the rooms are laid out for simple, easy maintenance, they are still large and comfortable. Sweeping rooflines, vertical siding, window walls and a wrap-around sundeck combine in a home meant for relaxing and sunning.

The focal point of the interior is the large living/dining room. The exterior setting is made a part of the room because there are window walls on either end of the area, as well as two windows and a door on the long exterior wall. A brick-faced fireplace is centered on the long interior wall. A spiral staircase on one side of the room links this space with a second floor balcony that gives access to two bedrooms and bath.

Although this plan is basementless, a full basement is an option if the terrain permits. The stair access would be from the laundry room where the utility closet is located.

This distinctive design is geared to family enjoyment of carefree, year round living with all the conveniences and comfort found in homes costing much more.

TOTAL LIVING AREA: First floor   998 sq. ft.
                       Second floor   548 sq. ft.
                       Deck   690 sq. ft.

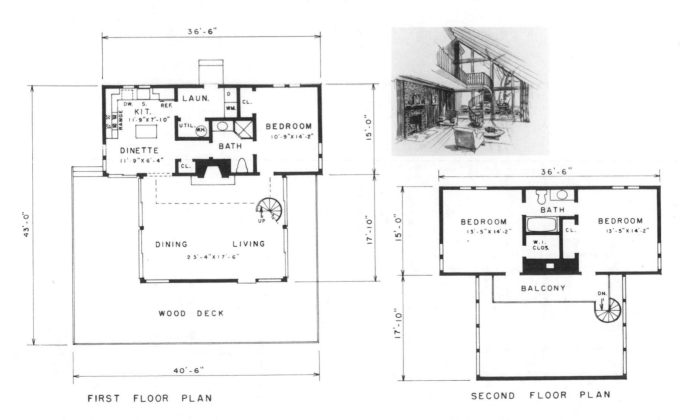

FIRST FLOOR PLAN

SECOND FLOOR PLAN

The Wexford

If your budget is tight, build this one-and-a-half-story, full-basement home as a two-bedroom, one-bath house and finish the upper level bedroom and bath later.

The main floor has both family living and entertaining areas. The living room has a beamed, cathedral ceiling and a large, corner fireplace. The kitchen, dining and family room areas are all one large, open space.

On the second floor, a study area is open to the living room below and has access to a rear sundeck through sliding glass doors. A bedroom with a large, walk-in closet and full bath complete this area.

TOTAL LIVING AREA: First floor   1,065 sq. ft.
                       Second floor   564 sq. ft.
                       Laundry   84 sq. ft.
                       Garage   308 sq. ft.

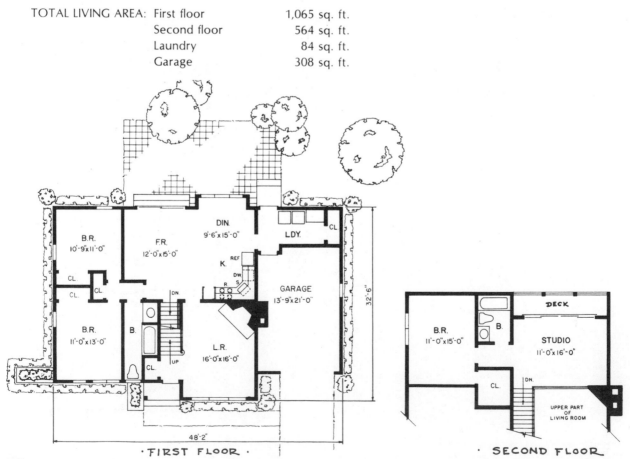

· FIRST FLOOR ·

SECOND FLOOR

The Lakeside

Here is a leisure home that will fit into either a woodland or shoreland setting. The major architectural features of this vacation or year-round home are the soaring butterfly roof, the vertical and horizontal beveled redwood siding, large expanses of glass and the large, cantilevered sundeck that extends along two sides of the house. The deck is ideal as a warm weather entertaining center. The high, peaked corner window wall is a dramatic accent to the exterior and to the sunken conversation pit/living room. The glass permits sunshine to fill the insides and creates a link with the outdoors.

Whatever your family leisure activity, this house, with its natural wood exterior and interior finishes, requires a minimum of maintenance and is designed to meet all recreation and relaxation needs.

TOTAL LIVING AREA: First floor   1,292 sq. ft.
Second floor   708 sq. ft.
Basement   612 sq. ft.
Garage   564 sq. ft.

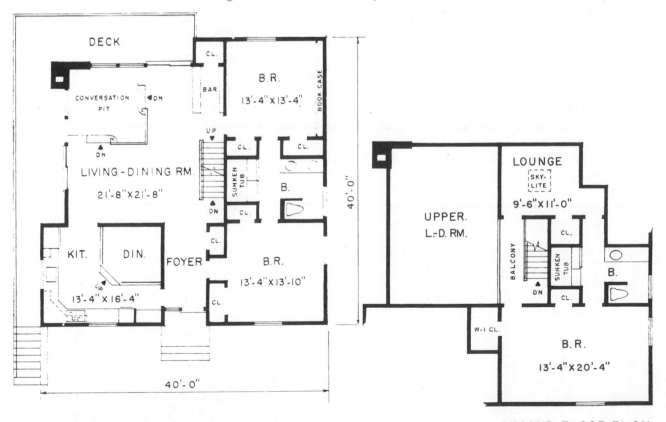

FIRST FLOOR PLAN

SECOND FLOOR PLAN

DOME HOMES

Introduced about 20 years ago, this unique concept of living is today enjoying new phenomenal popularity.

Technically, the dome home originated from the sphere, nature's most favored and efficient means of enclosing unobstructed floor space economically.

Due to inflation and the continued ever increasing building construction costs and the fact that the factory assembled triangular space frames are simply bolted together on the site to form the finished building, drastic reductions are possible on quantities of building materials and on-site labor costs. As much as 20 percent less for a dome home than for conventional housing.

The dome provides a living area that also answers the need for efficient energy consumption and is particularly adaptable to solar heating.

Today's dome homes are attractive and offer an exciting new way of living. The minute you step inside the front entrance you are surrounded by fascinating forms and deceptively large spaces.

Because air naturally travels in a circular pattern, heating and/or cooling a dome home is more efficient and economical.

The dome provides maximum enclosed space with minimum surface area which means efficiency in terms of heat-gain or heat-loss. It has been estimated that heating and cooling costs can be reduced by at least 25 percent.

Americans are shedding the conservative trappings of their urban life and are adopting a more youthful, modern and exciting life style.

The four dome home designs on the following pages will be of great interest to you . . .

The Futura

This prefabricated, standard-shell dome home is sold in a kit that is geared to the do-it-yourselfer. The kit can be assembled easily in just a few days by one or two persons using ordinary household tools. The dome can be set on a ground-level concrete slab or, if a basement or crawl space construction is desired, on floor beams. Because the shell is self-supporting, you can subdivide the interior space any way required.

Whether you are considering a small vacation home or a personal retreat, this 26-foot diameter model may be the best and most economical choice. Sliding glass panels at the front and rear of the dome provide a panoramic view. Skylights capture the sun during the day and the stars at night.

TOTAL LIVING AREA: 485 sq. ft.

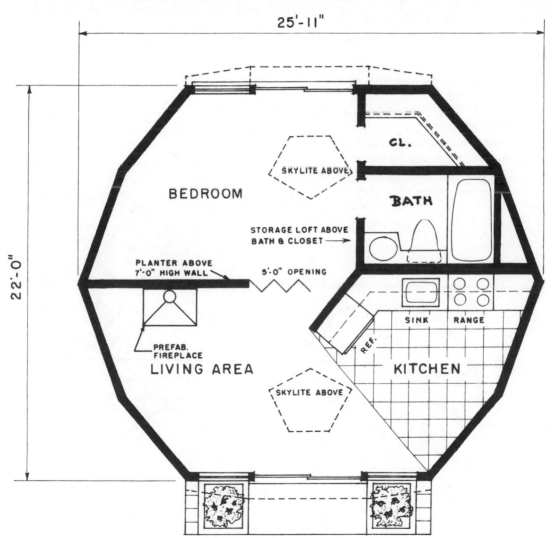

FLOOR PLAN

The Pentagon

This design in today's "dome homes" is among the best bets in efficient and economical housing. With the den used as an alternate second bedroom, the step saver kitchen, full bath and spacious living-dining area—you have all the space you need for a year-round residence, a vacation home in the mountains, on a lake, or at the ocean. If you desire—the second level may be omitted to save construction costs and increase the marvelous feeling of dome space living.

AREA: Ground Floor   1,085 sq. ft.
          Loft   380 sq. ft.

GROUND FLOOR PLAN

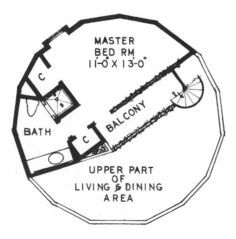

LOFT PLAN

The Leisure-Dome

If you have not stepped into the inside of a dome home, you are in for a real surprise.

Today's dome homes are attractive and offer an exciting new way of living. The minute you step inside the front entrance, you are surrounded by fascinating forms and deceptively large spaces.

In this design the dominant exterior architectural feature is the butterfly-roofed porte cochere that is screened by the decorative fieldstone wall and water fountains; but, by far the most dramatic space in the home is the panoramic living-dining-balcony space topped off by gigantic pentagon skylights that let the starlight in and show the clouds drifting by.

A decorative metal circular staircase provides ready access to the upper balcony that overlooks the living area below and leads to the master bedroom suite.

If an exciting new way of life is of primary importance, make a comfortable transition from a flat-ceiling, vertical wall home to a dome type residence.

AREA: Ground Floor   1,135 sq. ft.
         Loft   385 sq. ft.
         Storage Area   56 sq. ft.

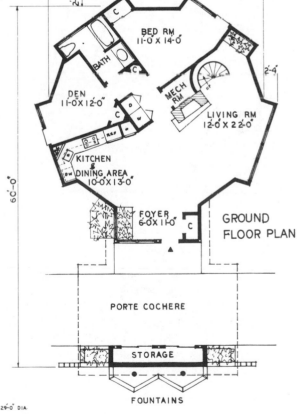

GROUND FLOOR PLAN

LOFT PLAN

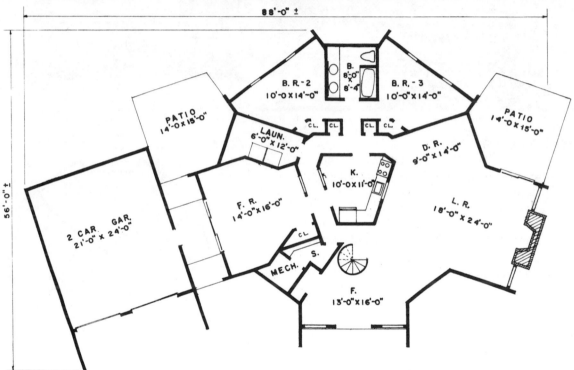

FIRST FLOOR PLAN

The DaVinci

A geodesic dome home is today's most advanced building concept. This dome home is spacious, and the design produces unusual and spectacular structure. If you feel comfortable with the unique, you will enjoy a distinctive home which, in the face of escalating construction and energy costs, is extremely practical. Initial construction costs are lower than for standard construction, and maintenance is minimal.

A family that enjoys being daring will find this home a pleasing, comfortable and efficient residence.

TOTAL LIVING AREA:		
	First floor	1,862 sq. ft.
	Second floor	695 sq. ft.
	Garage	550 sq. ft.

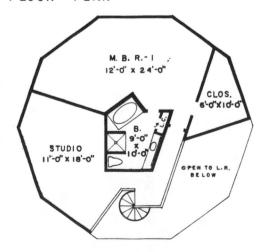

SECOND FLOOR PLAN

A HOUSE PLANNING GUIDE
FROM A TO Z

A After you have chosen your building site, obtain the services of a land surveyor to provide you with a topographical survey of your property. The survey should include grade contours, lot lines (their direction and length), location and depth of sewers (if available), water main, gas, electric, etc. All easements, existing trees and other physical property characteristics should be clearly indicated.

B Before beginning preliminary sketches, it is recommended, that copies of all rules and regulations governing the building activity of your area be obtained. This includes a local building code, local zoning restrictions, fire underwriters regulations, local, city or state sanitary requirements, etc.

C Committing yourself to a construction contract for the erection of your home is a matter of great and serious concern. If you do not have the cash necessary to pay for the entire construction cost, a building loan will be needed. A building loan or mortgage may be obtained from your local bank, building loan companies, savings and loan associations, insurance companies, mortgage firms or private individuals. A long term amortizing mortgage with monthly installments arranged like rent is the most convenient. These installments include interest, insurance, payment on principal and frequently taxes and water.

D Design your house to be in harmony with those in the neighborhood. Strive for architectural appeal by simple lines that will lend dignity to the structure. A well designed house gets a high mortgage rating.

E Economy in placing one bath over or adjacent to another is desirable, but this calls for discretion. An apparent saving of say $100. in plumbing might be more than offset in square foot loss and could inconvenience the circulation or convenience of the occupants.

F For an accurate estimate of the cost of your home, submit your plans and specifications to a builder or contractor. Cost per square foot is a good "rule of the thumb" figure but may vary depending on special built-in features, building codes, etc.

G Good residential design requires sound imagination, thought, originality and experience that can only be obtained from an architect. If you intend to use stock plans to construct your home, be sure they are the work of an architect, not a designer.

H Have the title searched on your property. This will protect you as the owner. When the title has been cleared you will get a deed which should be recorded in the proper court.

I If you wish to maintain the value of your property through the years, select a lot where the zoning ordinances have been established. They will protect your property against the encroachments of business, rooming houses, multi-family dwellings and other adverse influences.

J Just build a home to meet your immediate needs; don't go for too big a house. Don't expect to get all your ideas in one house but decide on a plan that is a compromise.

K Keep an open mind on new materials and methods. Consider building in several stages; what you need, build now; what you might need, build later.

L Land is scarce and getting more so every day. You will pay more for land today than it cost several years ago and chances are that it will cost more in the future. When you have decided on the lot make sure you obtain an owner's title insurance policy.

M Modern residential building construction is a complicated job in which scheduling of the work of various sub-contractors is very important. Masons, plumbers, electricians, plasterers, tile setters, carpenters, etc., must be coordinated with each other to avoid time- consuming costly delays.

N Neighborhoods with houses of different syles and prices is good. Stay clear from areas that seem to have all the houses built from the same basic design.

O Once you have determined your own particular home requirements, (two, three or four bedrooms) the only other cost factors are the size of house in square feet, number of baths and lavatories and the amount of livability per square foot.

P Plan your house to fit the lot and avoid the costly need of changing the existing topography to fit the house.

Q Quite apart from the topography of your individual lot you should note the terrain of the surrounding land. Proper drainage of your lot as well as the adjacent property is of utmost importance.

R Recommendations on good building contractors should be obtained from your architect, lawyer, real estate broker, lumber dealer, building supply house, bank or other lending institutions. Ask these builders for a list of the houses they have recently completed and it may be worth your while to visit and talk with some of the people whose homes they built.

S Select a local reputable contractor or builder, and make only written agreements in order to avoid future misunderstandings.

T Trick designs adversely affect the value of your property. It is unwise to build a home that is radically different in an "established" neighborhood.

U Unless you have unlimited funds and can afford to experiment and make mistakes, do not accept radical architectural designs, untried new materials and mechanical equipment. Unless you have a background in the building field, don't count on saving money by trying to act as your own general contractor.

V Visit your lot several times on different days and under different weather conditions. Carefully check the surrounding neighborhood and the orientation of the lot. A pleasant view adds to the enjoyment of life; a viewless lot, however, can be greatly improved by anyone with a talent for landscaping and gardening.

W When you apply for a loan, the bank or other lending institutions will want to know exactly where and what you intend to build. Bring along a copy of your house plans and specifications, a plot plan and a legal description of your property. Be sure you are prepared to establish your financial responsibility.

X Extraordinary precautions should be exercised in establishing your cost limitations. Your home may represent THE largest investment you will make in your lifetime. There is no substitute for good planning, good materials, good workmanship and safe and sound financing.

Y Your first step in building your home should be to consult a lawyer. His fee is moderate and his services, priceless. Explain your proposed building program to him. He will advise you about local procedures and will protect you from making costly mistakes every time you sign your name to a contract agreement.

Z Zoning regulations control what you can build on your lot and are a definite protection for the homeowner, because they keep commercial and industrial neighbors out of residential areas and thus tend to hold up real estate and property values.

WHICH HOUSE FOR YOU? CONSTRUCTION COSTS, AND MORTGAGE FINANCING

Once you have determined your requirements and made up your mind to build your new home, it will be easier to make further decisions. Whether the design you select is a ranch, split-level, or two-story, you should not confuse the architectural features with the style designation such as colonial, French, Tudor, farmhouse, etc. that may be adapted to any house.

There is endless debate on the relative merits of ranch, split-level, and two-story homes. Evidence can be produced by advocates of each style to show that their favorite offers more all-around economy, livability, and other virtues.

Rectangular perimeters are the least expensive to construct and simple straight roof lines are the most economical cover. Given a fixed area and price, a small rectangle is the least expensive one-story building; a two-story house with the same size foundation and roof would give double the living area but at less than double the cost. A split-level of the same original foundation size would increase the living area over the one-story. This is usually accomplished by "lifting" the bedroom area so that the basement floor below comes up to grade level, thereby providing additional living space on-grade in space that had been previously below ground. This "lifting" process causes some extra expense in framing and roofing, but it provides extra living area at less cost than could be obtained in a one-story building unless a larger foundation area and a rambling "L," "U," or "T" shape were given to the ranch.

The debate cannot be resolved on the basis of construction cost alone. Other features are desirable and are important in affording comfortable and convenient living. All agree that there should be definite separation between living, sleeping, and recreation areas. The controversy is whether this separation should be horizontal or vertical. The ranch house can provide this separation by good planning of the interior. This is difficult with the simple, basic rectangle. It is easier to design a bedroom wing and a recreation wing if each can extend away from the central core of living area. When stairs are no objection, the two-story layout provides this separation definitely and satisfactorily. In the split-level or other multi-level

arrangements, there are usually three basic living levels. Each is separated by a short flight of stairs. A fine degree the separation between living, sleeping, and recreation areas is provided by a separate level for each.

In this age the streamlined look seems appealing to many people even though they strive to obtain the character inherent in the colonial architecture. A two-story house would have to be large to obtain this effect, and would have a stately, rather than streamlined, appearance. The ranch or one-story home can have this pleasing effect even though small.

Split-levels are highly adaptable to many exterior styles. Arrangements of roof line and adjustments of levels can give two-story as well as ranch-like character to the conventional split-level home. The front-to-back and back-to-front split-levels can strongly suggest a ranch-type home and a two-story home, respectively. The conventional split-level suggests a house of separate wings, each for its own specific use. This is generally considered to be a sign of an expensive home.

Economy in heating and plumbing is another feature strongly debated by advocates of the different types of homes. The lower level recreation area of the split-level has long been a problem to properly heat. The introduction of the two-zone, forced-warm-air heating system has eliminated this to some extent. Concrete slab floor construction has some advantages when using hot water heat, however. The installation of hot water piping in the concrete results in a warm floor and radiant heat to provide the most comfortable winter area in the house.

Of course, proper insulation is a vital factor for economy of operation of any heating system. Naturally, exterior walls and ceilings at unheated attic areas are "must" locations for insulation. The most economical plumbing arrangements concentrate pipes in one small area. Small homes have baths located next to the kitchen resulting in less separation between sleeping and living areas. Good hall arrangement can compensate for this proximity somewhat, but for complete separation in the ranch plan, separate plumbing areas can be expected and these will increase costs.

HOME FINANCING:

Owning your own home has been greatly simplified during the past thirty years. Until the late 1970's the modern long-term, low-interest, self-amortizing mortgage (covering principal, interest, taxes, and insurance) made homeownership relatively simple. Under this plan the prospective homeowner makes regular monthly payments on the money that is borrowed. The real estate taxes and the interest you pay on your home are tax deductible. Recent changes in the economy have altered this somewhat.

The most common types of mortgage loans are conventional, VA, and HUD (U.S. Housing & Urban Development).

Conventional loans are usually obtained through the banks and other institutions. Since there is only so much money to lend these days, these institutions are trying to make the best of the situation by getting more and more selective, at interest rates higher than for FHA or VA loans.

The Federal Housing Administration (HUD) does not make mortgage loans. Instead, it insures the mortgage loans made through some 30,000 lending agencies. This protection enables lending institutions to make insured mortgage loans on competitive terms, with a small down payment and government-controlled financing rates.

The Veterans Administration also guarantees GI loans through regular lending institutions. If you are an ex-serviceman or woman, you may qualify for a lower down payment and a longer-term mortgage than civilians who have not served in the armed forces.

From time to time the government varies both the percentage of down payments required, the maximum number of years the mortgage may run, and the prevailing interest rate. Check with your local lending institution to see what rates are current before you start.

CONSTRUCTION COSTS:

There are several methods of estimating the approximate costs of any new home. The one most used by architects, builders, and appraisers is the square foot method. Cost of both materials and labor vary in different geographic locations. Local building conditions and codes differ to such a wide degree than an accurate unit scale is almost impractical. Generally speaking, construction costs range upward from $30.00 a square foot of living area, assuming that the work is done by a contractor. Any work that you may do yourself, such as painting, decorating, landscaping, etc., would reduce the cost.

Remember that only your builder can give you an exact and final building cost figure. The "rule of thumb", as outlined above, is merely for your generalized consultation. By multiplying the square foot area by the construction estimate, you will be able to estimate the cost of a home plan that interests you. (The cost of land, of course, will be entirely separate.)

SELECTING A BUILDER:

To build the home you have selected requires the services of a reliable contractor. If you know someone who had a home built and was satisfied ask for the name of the contractor.

Since you will definitely want to obtain several bids, interview several contractors, and, if possible, visit some of the homes that they have built during the last few years.

Many builders belong to the National Association of Home Builders. Although the NAHB is a national organization which officially credits home builders with a certain level of professionalism, a small builder (one who builds only two or three houses a year) may not belong, but still be competent and reliable.

Finally, do not sign any papers or agreements except in the presence of a lawyer. His services can help you avoid extremely costly mistakes in dealing with the builder, title company, or money lending institution.

HOW TO BUILD YOUR HOME

Your first step in building your home should be to consult a local lawyer. His fee will be moderate and his services, priceless.

Both husband and wife should attend when the lawyer is involved in discussions and paper signing. Explain your proposed building program to him. He will advise you about local procedures; he will protect you from making costly mistakes, and he will be on hand every time you sign your name to a contract or agreement.

BUYING PROPERTY

In most cases, you will be unable to obtain mortgage financing without ownership of the property on which your house is to be built. So this is the next step.

When you have found a lot which meets all your requirements, call in your lawyer. He will determine whether you really will be the owner of the land you are ready to pay for. The seller must be able to furnish you with a "clear title." Your lawyer will advise you how to proceed on this.

While this title search is going on, a prudent way to protect your interests is to have the deal held in escrow. That means turning the purchase price over to a third party (your own or the seller's lawyer, the real estate broker, your bank, or the title company) until the title is cleared. Once the deal is in escrow, you can proceed with the plot survey. Engage a local surveyor or civil engineer, because he probably has done other work in the neighborhood and may have time-saving data on file in his office, which will be reflected in his fee.

A complete plot survey shows on paper every outline, every angle, every dimension of your plot. The location, size, and depth of underground sewers, water mains, and gas lines should be plotted with the house connection stubs, if any. The survey should show the location of adjacent houses, if any, nearest your line on either side to permit placing your house to secure maximum privacy, light, and prevailing breezes.

A plot survey includes permanent markers on the ground on every corner and at every angle if the plot is irregular.

While your title is being searched, arrange to take out a title guarantee policy. It usually is cheaper to get an owner's title insurance policy from the company making the title search in connection with the sale. This is because the search and examination will not have to be duplicated, and the cost of this loss-prevention work on the part of the company accounts for the bulk of the title policy charge.

The biggest advantage to you in title insurance is that the title company must defend any claim made against your ownership. The cost of such a defense could exceed the cost of your whole home. The fact that the mortgage lender will also carry title insurance is not adequate for you; his covers the amount of the mortgage; your title insurance must also protect your equity over the amount of the mortgage.

When your title has been cleared, you will get a deed. Have this recorded in the proper court. You will pay a revenue stamp tax on the purchase price.

You have now acquired the site. It is protected against trouble. You are now ready to build your new home.

ARRANGING A LOAN

Rarely do families have the amount of cash necessary to pay the entire construction cost of the home; you will probably need to borrow money to build. What you need is a building loan.

This building loan is usually converted automatically into a mortgage when the house is completed. Terms of the mortgage will be established when you arrange the building loan.

Usually a builder will not start work without some down payment and an agreement on a schedule of payments to be made at regular intervals during the course of construction. Find out the financial requirements of the builder you select and establish whether he is to be paid directly by you or the lending institution. Your lawyer will help you. As a guide for your reference, here is a typical schedule of payments to the contractor while the house is being built:

10% on completion of foundation
25% on completion of the rough enclosure
30% on completion of the plastering, plumbing, heating, and electricity
25% on completion of the work
10% 30 days after completion of all work

Withholding of the final payment for 30 days is to insure correction of any defects or oversights. This should be mentioned specifically in your agreement with the builder which your lawyer will draw up for you.

HOW WARRANTY

Many builders now offer Homeowner Warranties with their buildings. This warranty protects the owner from any building failure in the first year. The warranty covers all parts of the structure and all installed materials.

At the time each payment is made to the builder, have your lawyer make certain that it is in accord with the original agreement and that you receive a proper statement of receipt. Before the final payment is made, your lawyer should carefully verify that the contractor has no liens or outstanding unpaid bills on this construction work that might become a claim against you.

It is usual to get a building loan and mortgage money from banks, local building and loan companies, or mortgage firms. These lending institutions are in business to make money and they have just one commodity for sale — money. There is real competition among lending agencies for your business. Do not hesitate to shop around

for terms that will be to your advantage.

Talk to a number of these representatives, but do not make out a formal application for a loan until you have studied their offers. Most homeowners find the long-term mortgage, with monthly installments arranged like rent, the most convenient. These installments include interest, insurance, payment on principal and, frequently, tax and water charges.

Interest rates vary. A fraction of 1% saved each year amounts to a sizable sum over the term of your mortgage. Depending on conditions in the money market, rates vary. Even though you may not need the biggest loan you can get, it is reassuring to know you could raise more funds.

Check to see how much the cost will be, if at some later time you might wish to pay off your mortgage because of a gift or inheritance, and after what period you can repay without penalty.

When you apply for a loan, the bank or other lending institution will want to know exactly where and what you intend to build. Be sure you take with you a copy of the house plans and specifications, and plot plan or short legal description of the property.

You must be prepared to establish your financial responsibility as a good risk. This means a statement of your assets and liabilities, income and employment record. A good "rule of thumb" is that 20% to 25% of your yearly gross income should equal or exceed your yearly payments on principal, interest, taxes, insurance, and maintenance of your home.

Here are some questions from a typical loan application form: what is your employment record, position held, salary, number of years on the job, previous positions with other firms, bank accounts, life insurance and amount of annual premiums, previous mortgage experience, stocks and securities held, other income, number of dependents, judgments or garnishments against your salary?

BUILDING PERMIT

A building permit is generally required before construction is started. Your builder may handle this for you or you may apply for it through your local building department. Two sets of house and plot plans are usually sufficient to submit with the application. One set will be returned with the building permit. A small fee is generally charged for the building permit.

MORTGAGE PAYMENT TABLE

Amounts shown include monthly payments of
interest and principal but not taxes and insurance.

20-YEAR MORTGAGE
(monthly payments, interest & principal).

Amount	9%	9½%	10%	10½%	11%	12%	13%	14%	15%
$16,000	144.00	149.15	154.41	159.71	165.15	176.17	187.45	198.96	210.69
20,000	180.00	186.43	193.01	199.68	206.44	220.22	234.32	248.70	263.36
24,000	216.00	223.72	231.61	239.62	247.73	264.26	281.18	298.44	316.03
28,000	252.00	261.00	270.21	279.55	289.01	308.30	328.04	348.19	368.70
30,000	270.00	279.64	289.51	299.52	309.66	330.33	351.47	373.06	395.04
36,000	324.00	335.57	347.41	359.42	371.58	396.39	421.76	447.67	474.04
40,000	360.00	372.86	386.01	399.36	412.88	440.43	468.63	497.41	526.72
44,000	396.00	410.14	424.61	439.29	454.16	484.48	515.49	547.15	579.39
50,000	450.00	466.07	482.52	499.19	516.10	550.54	585.78	621.76	658.40
54,000	486.00	503.36	521.12	539.13	557.38	594.58	632.64	671.50	711.07
60,000	540.00	559.28	579.02	599.03	619.32	660.66	702.93	746.11	790.08
64,000	576.00	596.57	617.62	638.97	660.61	704.70	749.79	795.85	842.75
72,000	647.80	671.14	694.82	718.84	743.16	792.78	843.52	895.33	948.09
80,000	719.78	745.72	772.02	798.72	825.76	880.86	937.25	994.81	1053.43
85,000	764.77	792.33	820.27	848.64	877.37	935.91	995.83	1056.99	1119.24

25-YEAR MORTGAGE
(monthly payments, interest & principal)

Amount	9%	9½%	10%	10½%	11%	12%	13%	14%	15%
$16,000	134.27	139.80	145.40	151.07	156.82	168.52	180.45	192.60	204.93
20,000	167.84	174.74	181.75	188.84	196.02	210.64	225.57	240.75	256.17
24,000	201.41	209.69	218.09	226.61	235.23	252.77	270.68	288.90	307.40
28,000	234.97	244.64	254.44	264.38	274.43	294.90	315.79	337.05	358.63
30,000	251.76	262.11	272.62	283.26	294.03	315.97	338.35	361.13	384.25
36,000	302.11	314.54	327.14	339.91	352.84	379.16	406.02	433.36	461.10
40,000	335.68	349.48	363.49	377.68	392.05	421.28	451.13	481.50	512.33
44,000	369.25	384.43	399.83	415.44	431.24	463.42	496.24	529.66	563.56
50,000	419.60	436.85	454.36	472.10	490.06	526.62	563.91	601.89	640.41
54,000	453.52	471.80	490.70	509.86	529.26	568.75	609.02	650.04	691.64
60,000	503.52	524.22	545.23	566.51	588.06	631.94	676.69	722.26	768.49
64,000	537.09	559.17	581.57	604.28	627.26	674.07	721.80	770.42	819.72
72,000	604.22	629.08	654.28	679.82	705.68	758.33	812.03	866.72	922.19
80,000	671.36	698.96	726.98	755.36	784.10	842.59	902.26	963.02	1024.66
85,000	713.32	742.64	772.42	802.57	833.11	895.25	958.65	1023.21	1088.78

IS NOW THE TIME TO BUILD?

Perhaps you are asking yourself such questions as: Are we ready to build now? Can we go ahead this year? Or will next year be better?

For most families facing this decision, the best answer usually is to do it *now*. Due to our recent inflationary economy, the value of homes has doubled or tripled during the past twenty years, so the odds are that, due to economic realities, homes will continue to increase in value along with a rise in labor and material costs. Any long-term investment like a home must rise in value during an inflationary economy. If you postpone the construction of your new home for even as short a time as one year, you may well find that the cost will have risen by as much as ten percent.

More importantly, the decision to go ahead now will enable your family to start enjoying the better living and the enhanced security of a new home that much sooner. You can safely expect the home you build this year to be worth several thousand dollars more ten years from now. In the meantime, as a homeowner, you will be enjoying special income tax advantages because your payments for mortgage interest and real estate taxes are fully deductible. Finally, your payments of mortgage principal will each month decrease the amount you owe; by meeting your monthly payments, your equity grows as automatically as if you were making regular deposits in a savings account.

You will experience the increase in the value and equity of your investment at the same time you experience the psychological satisfaction of owning your own home. Building to meet your family needs will also make this a special and exciting family event.

Creative Financing

Not too many years ago, anyone with a good work record, moderate savings, and a good credit rating could get a loan from any bank, savings and loan, or other lending institution. Recent years, however, have changed the money market so drastically that this is no longer true. Even a good credit risk with a 50% downpayment may have trouble getting a conventional loan. It is sometimes harder to get a loan to build a home than to buy an existing home. Before you get discouraged, however, consider all the available alternatives.

FAMILY MEMBERS

Although owing money to a member of the family may create some domestic strain, a business-like loan between members of a family is both legal and practical. If you have a relative able to make a loan, do not hesitate to approach that person with a strictly business proposition. Such loans should be made on a contract basis with the terms and payback agreed upon in writing. You should see an attorney to draw up the papers.

INSURANCE COMPANIES

There are two possibilities in dealing with insurance companies. You may be able to borrow the cash value of your insurance at an interest rate substantially below bank rates. However, this will cut down on the amount of coverage, and you should arrange other insurance to pay back the borrowed funds in case of illness or death.

You may also be able to arrange a mortgage through the loan department of your insurance company. Although most insurance companies only invest in large, long-term mortgages on commercial construction, some may offer special consideration to policy holders. Check your policy and call your insurance agent.

CREDIT UNION

If the company for which you work has a credit union, you may find that this organization is more willing to provide mortgage funds than your bank. Credit union members frequently overlook all the options and privileges available to them. If you are a member and have been saving at your credit union for a period of time, you may very well be able to get a substantial mortgage and/or building loan at a very competitive interest rate.

UNION FUNDS

Union members also have a frequently overlooked possible source of mortgage or building funds. Although not all unions offer such features, many of the larger unions invest in commercial mortgages. Check with your union officials to see if your union has a fund available for home mortgages for their members.

COLLATERAL

Because it is always easier to get a loan on an existing building than on a proposed building, you may find that you have to raise the construction funds and build the home before you can get a conventional mortgage. In this case, you will have to look to other sources of loan funds. If you have stocks, bonds, or other valuable possessions such as artworks, antiques or jewelry, you may be able to borrow against these items for a short-term loan to cover construction. Once the building exists, you should have less trouble getting a longer-term mortgage.

VARIABLE MORTGAGES

Many of the lending institutions that offer mortgages today are not offering the conventional twenty- or twenty-five-year mortgages. You may find that you can get a mortgage for a much shorter term. You may also find that you are offered a long-term mortgage at variable interest rates.

Although it is harder to make financial plans with either these two mortgage packages, both provide a means of getting the home you want. Assuming you are realistic about both your needs and your potential income, you should be able to adjust to the variations.

A short-term mortgage means that you will not be building equity at a very great rate. However, most institutions that offer short-term mortgages will renew the mortgage at new terms at the end of the period — one to five years as a rule — so that you will not have to find a new mortgage. You will have to accept the terms of the new mortgage, however, each time the renewal comes up, until you can arrange a long-term loan.

The variable rate mortgage is a long-term mortgage. You will know when you sign the papers that the mortgage will be paid off in a specific number of years. However, each year the mortgage rate will be reviewed and adjusted to meet the current market. You will find that your mortgage rate moves up or, possibly, down each year. Currently there is a spread of nearly ten interest points between mortgages eight or ten years old and new mortgages. With the variable rate, your mortgage will be at the current rate.

OTHER ALTERNATIVES

There are other possibilities for finding mortgages funds. Consider what you will need and all the possible sources of funds available to you. You may be able to combine several different sources to get the funds you need.

If you currently own a home, you may be able to sell that house, which should have increased a value over its original cost, and arrange with the new owner to live in the house, paying rent, until your new home is finished. That way your existing equity is available to you for construction.

The company for which you work may also be willing to assist you by arranging for or giving you a loan. This has become more common since company transfers often create housing problems for families. More and more companies have become aware that the current housing market has made it difficult for their employees to find adequate housing. The result has been, in some cases, a policy of assistance to employees in finding financing for appropriate housing.

Once you have made up your mind to build, there is always a way to accomplish your goal. Do not be discouraged if the mortgage market does not seem flexible. Look into all possibilities and you will find your financing.

About Your Home . . .
Before You Write—Read!

**We welcome correspondence and are happy to answer your letters,
but why not save yourself time and effort?
Perhaps the answer to your question is here.**

Are cost estimates included or can you tell me how much my favorite house will cost to build?

• Construction costs vary so much from one section of the country to another that you will do better to get a set of blueprints of your favorite plan and obtain an estimate locally. Costs range upwards from $30 a square foot of living space, assuming that the work is contracted out. Our designs show the square feet of living area. Unless otherwise specified, this does not include porches, terraces, garages, etc., since many of these features are optional and, of course, cost less per square foot to build than the main dwelling. With our blueprints you can get actual local cost estimates from builders and arrange financing with a mortgage lending institution.

Will you make plan changes for us?

• In most instances, changes in dimensions, substitution of items, materials, etc., or minor alterations can be done by the contractor during construction. If the house plan calls for wood siding, it can be changed to brick, stone or other materials; only the width of the exterior walls must be adjusted for the difference. We furnish conversion details, otherwise the working drawings for our designs are available only as illustrated. If major changes are involved, you should consider ordering one set of blueprints and having them redrawn by your local architect.

Will you tell me where a particular house has been built so I can look at it?

• During the past thirty years, we have sold many thousands of our plans for homes that have been built throughout the entire country. Unfortunately, our blueprint buyers seldom give us any information as to where or when they expect to build. Our design illustrations are accurately drawn perspectives and, with the exception of the landscaping, the house will appear exactly as shown.

Will plans meet local building codes?

• Our plans have been engineered for sound construction, but as long as there are almost as many different building codes as there are communities, there are bound to be rare cases of conflict. There is no need for concern, however, inasmuch as any suggested changes can usually be done during construction without the necessity of new or revised plans.

Can I get blueprints "in reverse" with the living room, for instance, on the left instead of the right as shown?

• If you find that your favorite house plan would suit you — or your lot — better if it were reversed, we will, upon request, send one of the sets transposed as in a mirror. Even though the lettering and dimensions appear backward, they make a handy reference because they show the house just as it's being built in reverse from the standard blueprints — thereby helping you visualize the home better. For example, if you order four sets of plans, we will send one mirror image, and three in the original position so that you can read the figures and directions easily.

How many sets of blueprints should be ordered?

• The answer can range anywhere from one to eight sets depending upon circumstances. A single set of blueprints of your favorite design is sufficient to study the house in greater detail. If you desire to get cost estimates, or are planning to build, you may need as many as eight sets of blueprints. For building, a minimum of four sets is required, one each for: owner, builder, building permit, and mortgage financing. In many cases, local building departments require two complete sets of blueprints before they will issue a building permit. Check with your building department.

How is the low cost of your blueprints possible?

• If you had complete working drawings especially created by a personal architect, the design fee for an individual home could be eight to ten percent of the total construction cost, and could range from several hundred dollars up to several thousand, depending on how big and complicated the design is. When you use our architect-designed plans (prepared by and/or under the supervision of professional licensed architects), the cost is spread among other families planning to build the same house in various parts of the country and they are sharing the total costs with you. Our many years of practical home planning experience assure you of a well-designed, practical house which will stay younger longer and make you feel proud of owning the home of your dreams.

Do you furnish specifications or a description of materials?

• All of our working drawings are furnished with specifications and a suggested description of materials required to construct the house as illustrated.

MATERIALS LIST (Optional): With each order of blueprints you may receive, at extra cost, an itemized material list which shows the type, size, and quantity of materials which are required to construct your home. Many contractors and material dealers prefer, however, to make up their own material list to take full advantage of materials most readily obtainable at best prices locally, thus permitting the substitution of items to satisfy your personal preference.

Solar Energy Saving & Information Guidelines

During the past several years, many conflicting articles have been written about the use of either passive or active solar heating in home building construction.

Active solar heating, is achieved primarily through the use of solar collectors, usually located on the roofs of structures, that absorb the warmth of the sun's radiation and transfer this heat and energy, either through a liquid or air medium, to a central location within the building. This heat and energy is then stored in a heat exchanger storage tank in the case of a liquid system, or directed into hot air storage bins that contain heat absorbing materials and then into a furnace, in the case of a forced air system, to satisfy the heating requirements.

Passive solar heating, however, utilizes little or no mechanical apparatus to achieve the same results. Passive solar relies almost entirely on home design, heavily insulated construction, and site and sun orientation to accomplish heat retention and utilization. The use of the natural elements is extremely important. Deciduous plantings or the use of banked earth are used extensively to achieve much of the desired heating and cooling.

SITE ORIENTATION

The single most important factor in utilizing solar energy, along with proper insulation and sound construction, is site location and house orientation. For maximum efficiency a home should be designed and located on a lot so most of the liveable portion of your home has extensive glass (preferably double or triple glazed) exposed to the south. It is preferrable to have the rear elevation on the south side of a slope. This concept will permit maximum exposure to the sun's lower warming winter rays, and also allow less direct overhead sunlight to enter during the summer months. The northern and western exposures should be designed with a minimum number of windows.

Another extremely important factor, as previously mentioned, is sound construction, with a maximum amount of insulation used in roofs, ceilings, and under unheated floor areas. Many contractors have already changed to framing exterior walls with 2x6 studding in lieu of the traditional 2x4 studding to allow for 6 inches of wall insulation, instead of 4 inches. Also, 10 inches of insulation should be used in ceilings rather than the customary 6 inches.

LANDSCAPING

Proper landscaping takes careful thought so that in clearing the construction site, any existing deciduous trees near the home site be left in place and not disturbed. With this type of planning, these trees can provide an excellent sun shield in the summer months and allow full sunlight to filter through the barren branches during the cold winter months.

Of course, the particular area of the country in which you live influences whether or not the added costs are advisable and practical. One authority has recently mentioned that, using present solar technology, about one-third of the area in the U.S. is compatible to use to total solar home construction. With this in mind, you must consider two very important factors before deciding whether or not to utilize a total active solar heating system in your new home; the additional investment and the practicality.

There is no question that a specifically designed solar home, either active or passive, will produce considerable savings in energy costs to the owner over an extended period of time. However, the question is will the investment pay for itself when you consider the overall savings including the cost of the original investment, the interest on that original investment at current interest rates, the savings on the implementation of a total solar heating system over the use of a conventional system, and expected length of stay in that dwelling.

If you live in an area of the country that has cold winters, many cloudy days, and rainy weather, then, you will also have to install conventional heating and hot water units as a back-up to the solar system. Since a complete solar system can cost as much as $10,000, one could well double that price for dual systems. Therefore, one must take the $10,000 solar system figure and multiply it by the current annual interest yield on that sum and then compare that figure with your overall savings on utilizing such a system over a conventional one to determine whether solar is justifiable. Compare this figure with what it currently costs you to heat your home, including hot water.

We feel that active solar energy is definitely an alternative to the future world energy problems, but that because of its present initial high costs of installation, and as yet infant stages of technology that currently exist, make it less appealing than passive systems. The spectrum of passive solar energy, combined with traditional sound home construction, strict adherence to the proper use of wall, window, and door insulation, attention to site location, and glass orientation is a more advantageous and desirable type of home construction. However, one should realize that the installation of solar systems need not be limited to the time of actual construction, but may well be implemented and adapted at a later date to any type or style of architecture with a minimum of effort.

The homes in this book have all been designed with this thought in mind, and include special solar energy details and information that can be utilized during the construction of your home.

Plan Orders
Mailed Within
24 Hours!

HOW TO ORDER YOUR BLUEPRINTS

If the design you have selected satisfies your requirements, mail the accompanying order blank with your remittance. However, if it is not convenient for you to send a check or money order, merely indicate C.O.D. shipment.

We will make every effort to process and ship each order for blueprints the same day it is received. Because of this, we have deemed it unnecessary to acknowledge receipt of our customers' orders. See order coupon below for the postage and handling charges for surface mail, air mail and foreign mail. Should time be of the essence, as it sometimes is—

For Immediate Service
Phone (201) 376-3200

Your plans will be shipped C.O.D. Postman will collect all charges, including postage. (No C.O.D. shipments to Canada or foreign countries).

NATIONAL HOME PLANNING SERVICE
37 Mountain Avenue
Springfield, N.J. 07081   Phone Orders (201) 376-3200

PLEASE SEND HOME DESIGN, BUILDING PLAN NAME: THE _____

First set of plans (if only one is desired) including specifications	$ 105.00	$ _____
Each additional set with original order @	$ 30.00	$ _____
Itemized & quantity Materials list	$ 25.00	$ _____
To have Plans Reversed (in addition to Cost of Plans)	$ 10.00	$ _____
Four (4) sets of Architect's Total Blueprint and Building Package including specification	$150.00	$ _____

ADD THE FOLLOWING POSTAGE:

First Class	$ 6.00	$ _____
C O D (U S Only)	$ 7.00	$ _____
Canada and Foreign Air Mail	$ 11.00	$ _____
Make payment in U.S. currency to National Home Planning Service	TOTAL AMOUNT	$ _____

MAIL ORDER TO:

NAME _____

STREET _____

CITY _____ STATE _____ ZIP _____

TELEPHONE #: AREA CODE _____ # _____

NATIONAL HOME PLANNING SERVICE

37 Mountain Avenue

Springfield, N.J. 07081   Phone Orders (201) 376-3200

PLEASE SEND HOME DESIGN, BUILDING PLAN NAME: THE _____

First set of Plans (if only one is desired) (including specifications)	$105.00	$ _____
Each additional set with original order _____@	$ 30.00	$ _____
To have Plans Reversed (in addition to cost of plans)	$ 10.00	$ _____
Itemized & quantity Materials list	$ 25.00	$ _____
Four (4) sets of Architect's Total Blueprint and Building Package (including specifications)	$150.00	$ _____

ADD THE FOLLOWING POSTAGE:

First Class Mail	$ 6.00	$ _____
C.O.D. (U.S. Only)	$ 7.00	$ _____
Canada and Foreign Air Mail	$ 11.00	$ _____

Make payment in U.S. currency to:

National Home Planning Service   TOTAL AMOUNT $ _____

Price subject to change without notice!

MAIL ORDER TO: (Print or Type)

NAME _____

STREET _____

CITY _____ STATE _____ ZIP _____

TELEPHONE NO.: AREA CODE _____ # _____ FMC 3

NATIONAL HOME PLANNING SERVICE

37 Mountain Avenue

Springfield, N.J. 07081   Phone Orders (201) 376-3200

PLEASE SEND HOME DESIGN, BUILDING PLAN NAME: THE _____

First set of Plans (if only one is desired) (including specifications)	$105.00	$ _____
Each additional set with original order _____@	$ 30.00	$ _____
To have Plans Reversed (in addition to cost of plans)	$ 10.00	$ _____
Itemized & quantity Materials list	$ 25.00	$ _____
Four (4) sets of Architect's Total Blueprint and Building Package (including specifications)	$150.00	$ _____

ADD THE FOLLOWING POSTAGE:

First Class Mail	$ 6.00	$ _____
C.O.D. (U.S. Only)	$ 7.00	$ _____
Canada and Foreign Air Mail	$ 11.00	$ _____

Make payment in U.S. currency to:

National Home Planning Service   TOTAL AMOUNT $ _____

Price subject to change without notice!

MAIL ORDER TO: (Print or Type)

NAME _____

STREET _____

CITY _____ STATE _____ ZIP _____

TELEPHONE NO.: AREA CODE _____ # _____ FMC 3